CALLED

"You hold a treasure in your hands. While we can't all walk with Kevin Cotter in person and on a daily basis, we can all walk with him through this book for the next five weeks. We can all allow him to be a mentor who guides us over this next month, but whose wisdom and insight will carry us far beyond one simple month and into eternity."

From the foreword by **Fr. Mike Schmitz**
Director of youth and young adult
ministry for the Diocese of Duluth

"Kevin Cotter has given regular people like me an immensely practical guide to doing something I've always wanted to do but felt unqualified and unworthy of doing—making disciples. Anyone who loves Jesus can, and must, help others love him too. There is no looking back."

Patrick Lencioni
Author of *The Five Dysfunctions of a Team*

"Everyone is called to evangelize. But the first step is learning to walk with Jesus as a disciple. This engaging, practical guide is sure to inspire and encourage you on your spiritual journey from being a disciple to becoming a disciple-maker."

Edward Sri
Catholic author, speaker, and theologian

"If you think of your faith as a private matter that you should keep to yourself, this book will change your mind! Kevin Cotter combines his deep knowledge of the faith with his love of Jesus to inspire us all to take our spiritual lives to the next level and help others do the same."

Jennifer Fulwiler
SiriusXM radio host and author of *Something Other Than God*

"Kevin Cotter provides an anointed combination of practical tips, personal stories, and deep spiritual insights that will challenge, inspire, and motivate you to evangelize the world. Seriously, take this journey of discipleship with him and Jesus, you won't be disappointed."

Pete Burak
Director of i.d.9:16 young adult ministry

"An inspiring and extremely practical guide. Get your hands on this book and get as many copies as possible into the hands of your parishioners."

Rev. James Mallon
Author of *Divine Renovation*

"If you dare to call yourself a Christian today, you need this book. Kevin Cotter offers clear, reasonable steps in evangelization and discipleship. *Called* takes you step by step in becoming a closer disciple of Christ and a herald for the Good News!"

Leah Darrow
International Catholic speaker and
author of *The Other Side of Beauty*

"Kevin Cotter has spent the last fifteen years immersed deep in discipleship. You will find in these pages many rich insights to aid your efforts in becoming an everyday disciple—there is no greater commission than becoming a disciple of Christ and leading others into discipleship!"

Curtis Martin
Founder and CEO of FOCUS

CALLED

BECOMING AN EVERYDAY DISCIPLE IN A POST-CHRISTIAN WORLD— A FIVE-WEEK GUIDE

KEVIN COTTER

AVE MARIA PRESS AVE Notre Dame, Indiana

Founded in 1865, Ave Maria Press is a ministry of the United States Province of Holy Cross.

www.avemariapress.com

Paperback: ISBN-13 978-1-59471-851-9

E-book: ISBN-13 978-1-59471-852-6

Cover and text design by Brianna Dombo.

Printed and bound in the United States of America.

Library of Congress Cataloging-in-Publication Data is available.

To all the people who have invested in me over the years: my parents, Robert and Laura Cotter; my brother, Chris; and my sister, Kelly; as well as Jay Heck, Mike Higgins, Joe Passantino, Dave Staples, and Dr. Edward Sri.

Thank you for showing me what discipleship looks like.

CONTENTS

WEEK 4—EQUIPPED

WEEK 5—DISCIPLE-MAKERS

FOREWORD

"Hey, Father, who is your mentor?"

The voice on the other end of the telephone belonged to a man who is about thirty years older than me, owns his own successful construction business, and is an overall manly and quite intimidating guy.

"Ummm . . . I have a spiritual director," I offered.

"No, not a spiritual director. Someone who can show you how to be the kind of Catholic—the kind of priest—you don't yet know how to be."

"I guess I don't know," I said.

"Well, I was in prayer the other day and I thought, 'Fr. Mike needs to have a mentor,' so I figured I would call you and ask if you had one. And then I decided that, if you didn't have one, I was going to let you know that you need to get one!"

Those words struck a chord with me, and I have reflected on them often since that phone call years ago.

A mentor. I had always wanted a mentor. All the people I wanted to be when I was a kid had mentors: Robin had Batman, Luke Skywalker had Obi-Wan Kenobi, Daniel LaRusso had Mr. Miyagi. All these characters had someone they could *see* lived differently; they all had someone who was further down the road than they were who could help them become the people they did not yet know how to be.

It was frustrating not having someone to teach me how to throw a batarang or master the crane kick, but this frustration reached an all-time high when I encountered Christ.

Even though I was raised Catholic, like many people in my situation, I couldn't have cared less about Jesus or the Church when I was younger. That all changed when I was fifteen or sixteen years old. I encountered the need for Christ in my personal brokenness, and then I encountered *him* in his forgiveness given through the Sacrament of Confession (but that is another story for another time). I wanted more than anything to be a disciple . . . I wanted to be a great saint. But there was a problem.

The problem was, when I looked around for someone to show me how to live as a disciple, I couldn't find anyone. I figured that there were probably people at my parish who prayed, but I didn't know who and I didn't know what to ask them. I figured that there were people who knew how to read the Bible, but how could I talk with them? I felt as if I had finally discovered the entire reason why I was on the planet (to be a saint-making disciple), but I didn't even know how to be a disciple myself.

Later, when I heard that every Catholic has the call and the commission to evangelize (to share the faith we have with others), I was even more *inspired* . . . and even more *discouraged*.

I was inspired because I truly wanted to share my love for Jesus. But I was discouraged because I didn't know *how* to share my faith.

I needed a mentor.

Looking back, I realize that I needed someone like Kevin Cotter.

I've been honored to know Kevin for a number of years now. He is a man who has built his entire life around his relationship with Jesus Christ. Ever since our first encounter, I've noticed something different about him. While Kevin takes great joy in life (I've never seen him without a ready smile for every person he meets), he also has a depth that is striking.

As you will learn, Kevin has been living as a disciple of Jesus Christ for the majority of his life. He has also lived as a "missionary disciple" for almost two decades. He is intimately familiar with the ordinary struggles that every follower of Jesus encounters . . . as well as the extraordinary joys of allowing Christ to truly be the Lord of one's life.

When I talk with Kevin, I get inspired (but not discouraged). He has a way of presenting the way of the disciple that makes Christianity *possible* and *powerful*. He is a real mentor.

For years, Kevin has walked alongside people who are both new and old to the faith and shown them how to be both disciple and missionary disciple. He has taught many people how to listen for God's voice, how to pray with the sacraments, and how to grow in virtue—even in the midst of real interior and exterior brokenness. Kevin knows the battles that men and women go through when they choose Jesus, and he knows how to navigate those danger zones. The more I reflect on it, if I were inclined toward resentment, I would begin to resent that I didn't meet Kevin earlier!

You hold a treasure in your hands. In *Called*, you'll gain the knowledge and tools you need to spread the Gospel to the ends of the earth. You'll also be challenged to renew your relationship with Jesus Christ through short, soul-renewing daily meditations. You can't give what you don't have, and in this book, Kevin offers you the gift of a new encounter with Jesus as well as the tools to offer that same gift to others.

While we can't all walk with Kevin in person and on a daily basis, we can all walk with him through this book for the next thirty-five days. We can all allow him to be a mentor who guides us over this next month, but whose wisdom and insight will carry us far beyond one simple month and into eternity.

In Christ,
Fr. Mike Schmitz

INTRODUCTION

I'll always remember the moment I said yes. I was twenty-three years old. I knew what God was calling me to do, but I was scared to do it.

Let me help you understand this moment a little bit better. My wife, Lisa, and I were going through the most difficult year of our lives. I was a full-time graduate student in my second year studying scripture and had two part-time jobs. In my spare time, I was cramming for the GRE and applying to PhD programs. Lisa worked full-time for the brand-new graduate school that I was attending. She was the only full-time employee besides the professors and was responsible for any administrative work— from hosting donor events to producing report cards (including my own!) to any other possible task that was needed to get this fledgling school off the ground.

Oh, and did I mention that we had just had a baby? The summer after our senior year of college, Lisa and I got married, and twelve months later we had a beautiful baby girl. We were first-time parents living in a city without any help, and our daughter was not a good sleeper. We loved her dearly, but for a long time we wondered why God gave us a baby who didn't sleep well in the midst of all the important things we had to do. But now I realize that we were two parents who didn't know a thing about helping a baby sleep! Between sleep deprivation, our very full lives, and the intensity of deadlines at work and school, we were exhausted.

After I had spent almost two years in graduate school, my friend Thomas approached me with a job opportunity. He asked if I had ever considered being a missionary with FOCUS (the Fellowship of Catholic University Students). At the time, FOCUS was just starting to hire married people, and they were enthusiastic about me being a missionary on campus.

On the surface, it seemed like the exact opposite of our desires: our plan was for me to complete a doctoral degree so that I could become a college professor. A job with FOCUS didn't lead me in that direction, and in fact, I could have taken this job directly out of undergraduate school. All the time, energy, and suffering that Lisa and I had invested during the two years of my master's program would, it seemed, go to waste.

And there was this whole thing about fundraising a salary. Each FOCUS missionary fundraises their salary to cover all their expenses—food, shelter, insurance, everything. FOCUS missionaries reach out to their family, friends, and parish community and ask them to join in their mission through financial support. We had friends who had joined FOCUS and fundraised their salaries. It wasn't easy, and it could be downright frightening. For us, there would also be some shame that I wasn't obtaining a doctorate as I wanted. Now, I would have to go to our family and friends and tell each one personally about that decision. On top of that, I'd ask them for support in the form of an ongoing donation to help us. Sounds like fun, doesn't it?

When Thomas offered me the job with FOCUS, all these thoughts were on my mind. There was just one problem: I felt immediately called to be a FOCUS missionary. I haven't had this experience very often in my life, but my heart immediately said yes, and there was a deep conviction inside that it was the right thing to do.

Now came the hard part. I knew that it was the right thing to do, but I needed to convince my wife as well. And if you know my wife, she's no easy sell! Let's just say it was a heated conversation. I'll spare you the details, but many of the hesitations and fears that I mentioned above came out in our talks over the next few days.

Not only was my wife not enthused about the job, but I knew my parents wouldn't be too happy either. From past experience, I knew that they didn't like the idea of people fundraising their salaries and would wonder where my life and career were headed, especially because I wasn't just a midtwenties kid trying to figure things out but a husband and father who needed to provide for my family.

I also remember a chilling conversation with a seminarian, now a priest, during this time of discernment. Our graduate-school classes were held in the same building as the local seminary, and I had built relationships with these men over the previous two years. I told him that I was considering becoming a FOCUS missionary. He couldn't believe that someone like me who was a husband, a father, and would soon hold a master's degree would consider such a thing. He thought it was a stupid idea!

This seminarian was a former FOCUS missionary.

While not all of my conversations during this time were so disheartening, and while my wife and parents eventually came to support the decision, it was a rough process. After graduation, we joined FOCUS kicking and screaming. Lisa did most of the kicking, and as a result, I did the screaming!

We were FOCUS missionaries for more than a decade, but that doesn't mean that we forgot just how hard it can be to answer God's call. It's definitely easier said than done.

WHY DID I WRITE THIS BOOK?

Making the decision to live for Jesus Christ and his Church is hard in our post-Christian age. Whether you're called to be a full-time missionary or not, I believe we are all called to be everyday disciples—men and woman who authentically live out Jesus' call to evangelize the world in practical ways in the context of everyday life. We are called to follow him with all of our hearts and to be missionaries who seek to love, serve, and bring good news to the lost.

That is what this book is all about.

I want to convince you that being an everyday disciple is not just something you should do out of obligation but something you are made for—something you do not because you have to but because *love compels you.*

I shared my story to show just how difficult this can be in the real world. But it is also worth pointing out that I know I was only able to make this decision because of the countless examples of those who made courageous decisions for Christ (many of whom are in the dedication of this book). This book is filled with dozens of examples to help you do the same. I hope that you have other people in your life that model discipleship for you as well.

WHO IS THIS BOOK FOR?

Maybe some of you are just starting your walk with Jesus. You've begun to commit your life to him and want to learn more about how to follow him as a disciple. This book will expand your vision on how to be like Jesus.

Perhaps you are already living as an everyday disciple on a mission, but you want to go deeper. This book will inspire and equip you to reach others for him.

Or maybe you're someone who is leading others to Jesus and building them up to reach the world with the Gospel. This book will give you additional confidence and motivation to encourage and prepare others.

WHAT WILL WE COVER?

This book will take you on a five-week journey into the heart of Jesus' mission, which is to proclaim the Gospel and to inspire others to do the same. Drawing on my fifteen years of mission work on college campuses, in parishes, and in discussions with Catholic leaders, I've created this guide to introduce you to the fundamentals of Christian discipleship, particularly as they apply to our postmodern culture and your relationship with Christ.

During my time in FOCUS, I learned a lot about their WIN-BUILD-SEND model, which is modeled off of Jesus' own ministry.

Before someone is sent out as a disciple, it's important that they encounter and commit to a relationship with Jesus Christ and his Church (WIN). Then they need to be formed in the faith (BUILD), and finally, they need to be mentored as a leader so that they can share the faith with others (SEND).

In the first week, we look at WIN as we encounter Jesus in our hearts. Specifically, we examine how Jesus called his first disciples. Understanding what discipleship was in the ancient Jewish world, and how his disciples first encountered him, will help us encounter or reencounter the person of Jesus today.

In the second week, we look at BUILD and what it takes to be a disciple of Jesus. What basic ways of thinking and habits allow us to be followers of the one we are called to imitate?

Our last three weeks are all centered on SEND.

In the third week we look at a vision for evangelization. We explore questions such as, Why should we evangelize? What was Jesus' mission? How did the people in his time react to this mission, and what does this say about our world today?

In the fourth week, we consider how to equip ourselves to reach a postmodern culture that continues to move further from the faith. What can we learn from Jesus and the saints about how to share the faith with others?

In the fifth week, we examine the concept of disciple-making. How do we answer Jesus' call to "make disciples of all nations"? What other models of discipleship in the New Testament and the lives of the saints can we learn from? How can all of this relate to our own personal work as well as work within a parish?

While the book takes you through the process of WIN-BUILD-SEND, it's important to note that these stages don't have to occur sequentially. As South America Bishops' document *Aparecia* states, "Mission is inseparable from discipleship, and hence it must not be understood as a stage subsequent to formation."[1] You will see mission connected with each stage as you progress through this book.

HOW TO USE THIS BOOK

This book is designed to be read daily. The chapters are short and compact to allow you to get through them quickly each day while still learning something meaningful and applicable to following Jesus and making followers of him. If you already pray each day, these chapters can be worked into your daily meditation.

If you miss a day, don't worry about it. Just pick back up where you left off and keep going.

If you can, read this book with someone else. Discipleship isn't a solo activity; it is one that requires us to discuss and practice it with others, just as Jesus did. Find a mentor who can read it with you, or grab a friend to join you.

In the end, this book is a journey, and the most important next step is to start. Let's begin with the theme of encounter.

WEEK 1—ENCOUNTER

DAY 1—ANTHONY

In the third century, an eighteen-year-old man named Anthony lost his parents. After their death, he continued to take care of his little sister, but he had a desire to live for the Lord. On the way to church one day, he was thinking about how the apostles had rejected everything to follow the Lord. When he arrived at Mass, he heard what Jesus said to the rich young man: "If you would be perfect, go, sell what you possess and give to the poor, and you will have treasure in heaven; and come, follow me" (Mt 19:21).

Upon having this encounter, Anthony decided to sell all that he had. He gave some of the money to provide for his sister and the rest to the poor. He then went off into the desert to live a life dedicated entirely to the Lord. His faithfulness to Jesus became so powerful that people traveled from miles around just to talk with him. He performed miracles and healings, and his visitors went on to tell others about the man whom they met and the amazing works of God that he did. People began to chronicle his life in books, and the story of his life spread throughout the Roman Empire. He was eventually known as St. Anthony of the Desert, and his story would affect the lives of millions of people.

PONTICIANUS

About one hundred years later, four officials who worked for the emperor in Rome were on a break. They split off into pairs and took a walk around the city. Two of the men stumbled into a house belonging to poor Christians, and there they read a biography of St. Anthony of the Desert. His story moved them so much that one said to the other something along the lines of, "Why do we try everything to become friends with the emperor when we can be friends with God right here and now?"[1] They had an instant conversion to Christianity and decided to be like Anthony—giving up all of their possessions and serving the Lord as monks. In fact, at the time of their conversion, they were both engaged to be married, so they had to break it to their fiancées that they were becoming monks. How did their fiancées react? They were both so moved by the account that they decided to convert to Christianity as well and dedicated their virginity to the Lord.

When these two men returned to meet the other pair of officials, they described what had happened to them. They warned their friends not to stand in the way of their conversion. One of these friends, Ponticianus, was so struck by their story that he converted to Christianity as well.

How do we know this story about the Roman officials, their fiancées, and Ponticianus? Years later, Ponticianus recounted this tale to Augustine of Hippo. Except when he told Augustine, Augustine wasn't a Christian yet. Have you ever heard that famous St. Augustine quote, "Lord, give me chastity, but not yet"? That statement epitomizes St. Augustine's state of mind at this time in his life. He knew what he needed to do, but he wasn't willing to accept it in his heart. It was at this point that Augustine met Ponticianus. Ponticianus saw that Augustine had a copy of St. Paul's epistles, so he told him this entire story about St. Anthony and his coworkers and his conversion. While he was speaking, Augustine began to feel ashamed. Ponticianus's stories reminded Augustine of who he was supposed to be.

When they finished their conversation, Augustine went into his garden and wept. He heard a voice like a child repeatedly singing a Latin phrase, *Tolle lege, tolle lege* ("Take and read, take and read"). Taking it to be from God, Augustine recalled that Anthony's decision to go into the desert occurred when he heard the Gospel at Mass. He believed the voice was a divine command to pick up his book of St. Paul's epistles and read the first passage that he found. (Perhaps the first instance of Bible roulette.)

Augustine read, "Let us conduct ourselves becomingly as in the day, not in reveling and drunkenness, not in debauchery and licentiousness, not in quarreling and jealousy. But put on the Lord Jesus Christ, and make no provision for the flesh, to gratify its desires" (Rom 13:13–14). Augustine now had the answer he needed to break the bonds of lust in his life. At this moment, everything changed. Augustine went on to be one of the greatest saints and theologians that the Church has ever known. His autobiography is one of the most read books in the history of mankind. And his journey with Jesus and the Church all began with one man sharing his encounter with the Lord.

ENCOUNTER

The stories of Jesus, the rich young man, Anthony, Ponticianus, and Augustine are a great intro into this week and into this book. These stories speak to the rich tradition of how encountering Jesus can change everything. These encounters can cause us to decide to follow after Jesus and to share this encounter with others. If we seek to evangelize, then we must live out of an encounter with Jesus.

I know this has been true in my own life. My own intense encounter with Jesus just before high school caused me to make radical life changes, and I naturally began to tell others about my relationship with Jesus.

So often in FOCUS's work, students become missionaries because of an encounter they had with Jesus at a conference or in a Bible study that dramatically changed their life. On the flip side, so often when missionaries or others in ministry burn out, it is because they have stopped encountering Jesus. These experiences speak to a timeless principle—we can't give what we don't have. If we are receiving God's mercy, we are in a better place to give it to those who need it most.

That's what the first week of this book is all about. Jesus is calling you to follow him, but first we need an encounter with him for it all to make sense. During this week, we will consider Jesus' first encounters with his disciples and what they can mean for our encounters with Jesus today.

REFLECTION

When have you encountered Jesus? What did you do to continue to encounter him? How did these encounters change your life? Did it change how you talk about Jesus with others? How have other people's encounters shaped your own life?

DAY 2—FOLLOW

We can gain key insights into what it means to follow Jesus by reflecting on how his first disciples were called. Let's take a look at that moment.

> As [Jesus] walked by the Sea of Galilee, he saw two brothers, Simon who is called Peter and Andrew his brother, casting a net into the sea; for they were fishermen. And he said to them, "Follow me, and I will make you fishers of men." Immediately they left their nets and followed him. And going on from there he saw two other brothers, James the son of Zebedee and John his brother, in the boat with Zebedee their father, mending their nets, and he called them. Immediately they left the boat and their father, and followed him. (Mt 4:18–22)

We often don't ask enough questions as we read scripture, especially when we read stories about Jesus. Sometimes we think, "Oh, there goes Jesus again. People do crazy things around him because he is the Son of God and that's what he does!" But these were actual human beings who made real decisions based on what they saw. If we look at this story in a different context, perhaps that of our everyday life, it sounds pretty strange. You're busy working with your dad and brother, and a teacher comes along and says, "Come, follow me," and right then, you quit your job, leave your father in the dust, and follow some guy across the country. That would be pretty odd, right? Why are Peter, Andrew, James, and John all willing to drop their nets and follow Jesus simply because he asked them to?

JEWISH DISCIPLESHIP

Jesus didn't start the tradition of teachers and disciples; it was a part of the Jewish education system of the day. For the ancient Jewish people, education, and in particular the study of the Hebrew Scriptures, was their highest priority. It was how they passed their faith to the next generation.

Most Jewish children in Jesus' day started education at a school called Bet Sefer, or House of the Book, the equivalent of elementary school for those who were six to ten years old. During this time in a child's life, education consisted of one thing: memorizing the first five books of what we call the Old Testament—Genesis, Exodus, Leviticus, Numbers, and Deuteronomy.

At this point, most students stopped schooling. Instead, they learned their family's trade in preparation for a career. But the best and brightest from Bet Sefer would continue their education and go on to Bet Talmud, or House of Learning, from the ages of ten to fourteen. Here, they focused on memorizing and interpreting the rest of the Hebrew Scriptures.

If you were one of the best and brightest at the end of Bet Talmud, you presented yourself to a rabbi and entered Bet Midrash. The rabbis held an honored place in the Jewish culture because they taught the people how to read and interpret their sacred texts. To study under a rabbi and to have the opportunity to become a rabbi was like getting into Harvard or receiving a Division I scholarship to play football in our culture. The rabbi accepted the disciple by saying two Hebrew words that every Jewish boy wanted to hear: *Lek Hackeri*, or "Come, follow me."[2]

JESUS' DISCIPLES, THEN AND NOW

With all of this in mind, let's return to the passage where Jesus calls his disciples. First, instead of the disciples presenting themselves to the rabbi, Jesus goes to them. This is even more surprising because Peter, Andrew, James, and John are working their family trade. (So they aren't the best and brightest.) When they hear the words *Lek Hackeri*, or "Come, follow me," they must not believe Jesus at first. It would be like receiving an invitation to attend Harvard without making the honor roll, or a scholarship to play Division I sports when you never made the varsity team. Now we begin to see why they were so willing to leave everything behind. This was the opportunity of a lifetime, and they weren't going to miss it.

So what does this all mean for us today?

It means that you don't have to be a superstar to be Jesus' disciple. You don't have to be perfect—not even close! Peter, Andrew, James, and John weren't perfect. They were average— just like you and me. Yet Jesus called them to be his very first disciples.

And the reality is that Jesus calls you today. He wants *you* to be his disciple. Wherever you are right now, imagine Jesus walking into the room, looking you in the eye, and saying, "Come, follow me." What would this be like? How would you react? What would you change in your life to follow him? Because ultimately, Jesus is calling you and he believes that you—yes, *you*—have what it takes.

REFLECTION

Take some time to imagine what it would be like for Jesus to personally call you to be his disciple. What would he say to you? How would you react?

DAY 3—INADEQUATE

When we think of Jesus calling us to follow him, we may have a natural reaction—I'm not worthy! Many of us, including myself at times, think, "This isn't for me," or "I'm not made for this." When students are invited by FOCUS missionaries into leadership on campus, they often have this same reaction—"You've got the wrong person. I can't do this." In fact, this isn't just a natural reaction today; it was the early disciples' reaction as well.

The account of Jesus' calling of Peter, Andrew, James, and John that we discussed yesterday came from the Gospel of Matthew. The Gospel of Luke gives us a different version. Luke slows down the scene with Jesus and Peter and gives us more details.

> And [Jesus] sat down and taught the people from the boat. And when he had ceased speaking, he said to Simon, "Put out into the deep and let down your nets for a catch." And Simon answered, "Master, we toiled all night and took nothing! But at your word I will let down the nets." And when they had done this, they enclosed a great shoal of fish; and as their nets were breaking, they beckoned to their partners in the other boat to come and help them. And they came and filled both the boats, so that they began to sink. But when Simon Peter saw it, he fell down at Jesus' knees, saying, "Depart from me, for I am a sinful man, O Lord." . . . And when they had brought their boats to land, they left everything and followed him. (Lk 5:3–8, 11)

Despite his faithfulness to follow Jesus' command to put the fishing nets on the other side of the boat, Peter considers himself unworthy, noting his sinfulness. This same feeling can come over us as well. Doesn't Jesus know all the bad things that we've done? Doesn't he know my inmost thoughts and fears? My inclination to be selfish? My lack of devotion? My sinful nature? Why would Jesus want *me* to follow *him*? Doesn't he know that I'll mess up everything?

But Jesus makes himself clear: "If *any man* would come after me, let him deny himself and take up his cross and follow me" (Mk 8:34, emphasis added). Being a disciple of Jesus is open to everyone, and one of the key challenges that we need to overcome is our sense of inadequacy. Maybe the following story can help.

PLAYING PIANO

In the mid-nineteenth century, British aristocrat Lord Radstock, while staying in a Norwegian hotel, heard a piano being played horribly in the hallway downstairs. When he looked over the balcony, he saw a little girl making a dreadful noise on the keyboard. Normally, Lord Radstock was a patient man, but the racket began to drive him crazy. While he watched the little girl, a man approached the piano and sat down beside her. Instead of stopping the little girl's efforts, he began to play and construct chords right alongside her. Each of his keystrokes complemented her notes, and suddenly a breathtaking sound filled the hotel. He took her mistakes and discord and turned them into something beautiful.[3]

The question of our effectiveness in following Jesus doesn't come down to our performance or our gifts. As the story of the little girl playing the piano suggests, it relies on our relationship with our Father, who takes our weaknesses and faults and turns them into something beautiful.

This only happens if we are willing to live like him, even when we feel incredibly weak.

This only happens if we are willing to trust that our Father will do something with our attempts, no matter how inadequate they seem.

This only happens if we remain in relationship with our Father, and we don't run away out of fear, shame, or guilt.

As St. Paul has beautifully written, "But [the Lord] said to me, 'My grace is sufficient for you, for my power is made perfect in weakness.' I will all the more gladly boast of my weaknesses, that the power of Christ may rest upon me" (2 Cor 12:9).

PETER—THE IMPERFECT EXAMPLE

We see all of these dynamics in the life of St. Peter. Peter has many wonderful experiences during his time with Jesus, but there are also many times when Jesus must have put his palm to his forehead and asked, "Peter, what are you thinking?!"

It is Peter who, upon hearing of Jesus' plan to die on the Cross, attempts to stop our Lord from doing so, only to hear from Jesus, "Get behind me, Satan!" It is Peter whom Jesus specifically asks to pray with him during the Agony in the Garden, only to find the apostle sleeping. It is Peter who is adamant that he won't betray Jesus and then does so anyway—three times, no less!

After all of these mistakes, could you imagine facing Jesus? Think of all of the emotions that Peter must have felt after the Resurrection. To betray your best friend, your Lord, the one who appointed you to lead the Church, and then to encounter him in his glory—and yet Peter is still willing to face our Lord and be reconciled to him.

In John 21, the gospel writer records Peter's first one-on-one encounter with Jesus after the Resurrection.

> When they had finished breakfast, Jesus said to Simon Peter, "Simon, son of John, do you love me more than these?" He

said to him, "Yes, Lord; you know that I love you." He said to him, "Feed my lambs." A second time he said to him, "Simon, son of John, do you love me?" He said to him, "Yes, Lord; you know that I love you." He said to him, "Tend my sheep." He said to him the third time, "Simon, son of John, do you love me?" Peter was grieved because he said to him the third time, "Do you love me?" And he said to him, "Lord, you know everything; you know that I love you." Jesus said to him, "Feed my sheep." . . . And after this, he said to him, "*Follow me.*" (vv. 15–17, 19, emphasis added)

Notice Jesus' line of questioning. He doesn't ask Peter, "Do you know what you did wrong?" He doesn't say, "Depart from me, you wicked person!" He simply asks, "Do you love me?"

Both Peter and Judas betray Jesus. The difference between them isn't so much the sin that they commit against our Lord, but the fact the Judas lets his sin, guilt, and shame overcome his relationship with the Lord. While Peter very much experienced these effects, he desires to receive forgiveness and remain in Jesus' love. Upon hearing Peter's response to love, Jesus restores his relationship with him and at the same time utters the words from the encounter that began their journey together: "Follow me."

Everyone who seeks to follow Jesus feels inadequate at some point. There are moments when we don't believe we are worthy to follow our Lord. There are moments when we feel as if our sin and shame are too much to carry on. And yet the Lord asks one question if we are to continue to follow him: "Do you love me?" In the midst of our inadequacies, Jesus gives us the opportunity to renew our love for him and to respond once again to his call to follow him.

REFLECTION

1. What inadequacies do you feel when you seek to follow Jesus? What weaknesses, faults, and sins come to mind?
2. How do these weaknesses, faults, and sins change your relationship with Jesus and with others? How do they prevent you from following him more closely? What opportunities do they give you to build up your relationship with Jesus?
3. Why is Jesus' question to Peter so important? While we need to ask for forgiveness and go to Confession, why is love the most important factor?

DAY 4—IDENTITY

As Jesus continued his ministry, he called more and more people to follow him. Soon people became suspicious of the kind of followers that Jesus had. The Gospel of Luke records one of these moments: "Now the tax collectors and sinners were all drawing near to hear him. And the Pharisees and the scribes murmured, saying, 'This man receives sinners and eats with them'" (15:1–2).

As we saw previously, rabbis (especially those as talented and wise as Jesus) called the very best to follow them. But the Jewish officials of Jesus' day noticed that many of his disciples were, well, seemingly inadequate. In response to this accusation, Jesus tells three parables: the lost sheep, the lost coin, and the lost son (commonly known as the prodigal son). With these parables, especially that of the prodigal son, Jesus tells a story that redefines how we should look at the identity of God and, in turn, our own identities as well.

The parable focuses on two sons. The younger son, the prodigal, goes to a faraway land where he squanders his inheritance on an immoral lifestyle. After he spends all of his money, a famine strikes and he is forced to be a servant. As he feeds the pigs, feeling hungry enough to eat their food, he comes to his senses and says, "How many of my father's hired servants have bread enough and to spare, but I perish here with hunger!" (Lk 15:17). The younger son realizes that life in his father's house is way better than the life he has in a foreign land. He's willing to be a servant just to be in his father's home again. His memory of his life as a son drives him to start the long journey back. Upon seeing him, the father runs to meet him and greets him with a ring and a robe, signs that he is welcomed back into the family. The father responds to him not according to the things he's done but according to his identity as a son.

Upon the younger son's return, we learn more about the older son.

He never left home, but his conversation with his dad about his younger brother reveals the kind of relationship they have. Not only does he refuse to join his father in rejoicing over his brother's return, but he also tells his dad, "Lo, these many years I have served you, and I never disobeyed your command" (Lk 15:29). This statement is certainly something that a son could say to his father, but it's also something that a servant or slave might say. He continues by saying that in return for his service, he has never received a reward: "Yet you never gave me a kid [baby goat], that I might make merry with my friends" (v. 29). The older son is protesting the injustice of his younger brother receiving a fattened calf while he hasn't received even a kid. In the older son's mind, the rewards don't match up with the service given.

The father replies, "*Son*, you are always with me, and all that is mine is yours" (Lk 15:31, emphasis added). With these words, the father redefines his son's understanding of the situation. The sons are not servants; they are family—this is their identity. He doesn't deserve a reward for his efforts; he owns everything with his father.

In the parable of the prodigal son, Jesus is correcting the vision that his audience and his early followers have of who God is and who they are called to be. Jesus is redefining God's identity and their identity as well. Just like Jesus' first audience, we need to convert our hearts and minds away from the culture we've been brought up in and change the way we think about who we are.

ARE WE THE OLDER SON?

Whether someone has converted to Christianity or been a Catholic their whole life, they can fail to understand their identity in light of who God is and who he calls us to be. Perhaps the best description of God's identity is the Trinity, a relationship of self-giving love. The Father completely gives himself to the Son, and the Son completely loves the Father, and through this love, we have the Holy Spirit. Through our baptism, the *Catechism of the Catholic Church* tells us, "We are called to share in the life of the Blessed Trinity" (*CCC* 265). This is in fact why Jesus became a man. In the words of St. Thomas Aquinas, "The only-begotten Son of God, wanting to make us sharers in his divinity, assumed our nature, so that he, made man, might make men gods."[4]

Our identity is that of sons and daughters of God. In a consumeristic culture, we've been programmed to think very differently. We live in a world of transactions. If I work hard, then I will earn what I'm supposed to get. If you do this for me, then I'll do that for you. Not only that, but we begin to identify ourselves with what we do. It's common to answer the question of who we are with what we do. I'm a lawyer. I'm studying economics. I've written a book. When our identity becomes synonymous with what we do, we no longer think like sons and daughters. The older son thinks it isn't fair that his brother gets the fatted calf after spending his inheritance on prostitutes when he's been obedient and doesn't even get a baby goat. The father is teaching an important lesson: you are both my sons, and that isn't something you can earn.

ST. THÉRÈSE

St. Thérèse of Lisieux, also known as St. Thérèse of the Child Jesus, teaches us what it means to be a son or daughter of God.

Her little way emphasizes the need to be a child of God, and she often makes her point with real-life examples.

> It is needful to remain little before God and to remain little is to recognize one's nothingness, expect all things from the good God just as a little child expects all things from its father. . . . Even among poor people, a child is given all it needs, as long as it is very little, but as soon as it has grown up, the father does not want to support it any longer and says: "Work, now you are able to take care of yourself." Because I never want to hear these words I do not want to grow up, feeling that I can never earn my living, that is, eternal life in heaven.[5]

St. Thérèse never wants to "grow up" because this will change her dynamic with God. Like a child, she wants to trust her Father wholeheartedly. Like a child, she wants to depend on him instead of relying on herself. So, if we don't have to "do" anything, what are we supposed to do? Like a child, we are called to respond with love. As St. Thérèse notes, "See, then, all that Jesus lays claim to from us; He has no need of our works but only of our love." This is the child who runs into her parents' arms because she knows she is loved, and she wants to respond with love. Children live with the freedom and joy of unconditional love. Living out of this unconditional love isn't easy. But when we learn to live from this identity, we encounter a Father who can change the way that we look at everything, including ourselves.

REFLECTION

Take some time to look at the chart on the next page and prayerfully reflect on the difference between son and servant. In what areas of your life do you struggle with seeing your identity correctly? What lies do you tell yourself about your relationship with God? What causes you to believe these lies?

IDENTITY	
SON	*SERVANT*
Identity is found in relationship	Identity is found in what we do
Relationship is unconditional	Relationship is transactional
The son becomes like the father	The servant never becomes the master
Response is of trust and self-giving love	Response is of fear and self-love

DAY 5—WOUNDS

Despite Jesus' desire to have us follow him and our identity as his sons and daughters, many of us carry deep wounds into our relationship with him. These wounds can be our own doing or the result of something that someone did to us. These wounds can prevent us from following Jesus and sharing him with others. They can hinder us from seeing God as a loving Father and recognizing ourselves as sons and daughters. But they can also provide a unique and powerful opportunity to encounter our Lord.

One of the most prominent aspects of Jesus' ministry is healing. In Matthew chapters 8 and 9 alone, Jesus heals a leper, a paralyzed man, Peter's mother-in-law from a fever, "many who were possessed with demons," two demoniacs, a paralytic, a young woman who has died, a woman with a hemorrhage, two blind men, and a dumb demoniac. It is clear that Jesus wants to restore us and that an encounter with Jesus' healing can profoundly change us.

Call to mind the deepest wound that you have in your own life, something you wish were healed. Keep this in mind as we break down one of the most compelling healing stories in Mark, the story of the blind beggar Bartimaeus, in chapter 10. As we look at his story, put yourself in Bartimaeus's position. Replace his blindness with your wound.

BARTIMAEUS

And they came to Jericho; and as [Jesus] was leaving Jericho with his disciples and a great multitude, Bartimaeus, a blind

> beggar, the son of Timaeus, was sitting by the roadside. (Mk 10:46)

First, it is unusual that Mark uses Bartimaeus's name in this passage. Almost every person who is healed by Jesus remains anonymous; even Peter's mother-in-law is not named. Also, "Bartimaeus" is an unusual name, a combination of Hebrew and Greek. *Bar* in Hebrew means "son of," and *Timaeus* means "honor." This "son of honor" looks like anything but this—he is a blind beggar by the roadside. For ancient people, blindness was akin to being dead. Eyesight was vital for staying alive and taking care of yourself; hence Bartimaeus has to beg to survive. In the book of Tobit, the main character becomes blind and cries out, "I am a man without eyesight. . . . Although still alive, I am among the dead" (Tb 5:10, NRSV). Knowing this background helps us to realize just how desperate Bartimaeus is. Often we feel trapped and held hostage by the wounds in our lives.

> And when he heard that it was Jesus of Nazareth, he began to cry out and say, "Jesus, Son of David, have mercy on me!" And many rebuked him, telling him to be silent; but he cried out all the more, "Son of David, have mercy on me!" (Mk 10:47–48)

His condition of blindness helps explain why Bartimaeus is so excited when he hears that Jesus is coming. Even though he can't see Jesus and doesn't know exactly where he is, this blind man begins to cry out to him. Despite the crowd's insistence that he stop, Bartimaeus "crie[s] out all the more." Bartimaeus realizes that Jesus is his only hope. He not only acts like it, but he also identifies Jesus this way: "Jesus, Son of David, have mercy on me!" The title "Son of David" is a messianic one. When Bartimaeus cries out, he is publicly declaring Jesus as the Messiah, the one to restore Israel (Is 35).

In our brokenness, we continuously need to claim Jesus' identity and our own. Jesus is the Son of God, our Messiah, our Savior, the one who died for us, the one who heals us. He is the one who restores us. As we claim his identity, we also need to claim our own. We are God's sons and daughters and are in need of his mercy. St. Augustine once said, "No matter how rich a man is on earth, he is still God's beggar." We need to be like Bartimaeus and cry out with faith, "Jesus, Son of David, have mercy on me!"

> And Jesus stopped and said, "Call him." And they called the blind man, saying to him, "Take heart; rise, he is calling you." And throwing off his mantle he sprang up and came to Jesus. (Mk 10:49–50)

Jesus hears Bartimaeus's cries and his claim that Jesus is the Messiah, and he calls the blind man to himself. Bartimaeus's reaction is telling; he throws off his mantle. For a blind beggar, his mantle was essential. It was what he slept on. It protected him from the elements. He would use it to collect alms. Bartimaeus has such trust in Jesus that he is willing to let go of his past life in a real, tangible way.

Like Bartimaeus, we need to be willing to leave our old selves behind. Bartimaeus throws off his mantle, an emblem of his lifestyle, *even before* Jesus heals him. Jesus can't heal our wounds if we continue to mask them with bandages. He can't apply his grace if we aren't willing to be exposed to his treatment.

Finally, we come to the end of our story.

> And Jesus said to him, "What do you want me to do for you?" And the blind man said to him, "Master, let me receive my sight." And Jesus said to him, "Go your way; your faith has made you well." And immediately he received his sight and followed him on the way. (Mk 10:51–52)

Jesus sees a blind man before him who wants mercy and yet he still asks, "What do you want me to do for you?" Bartimaeus asks for sight and receives it. Jesus heals him and lets him know that it was his faith that made him well. While we often think only of the apostles or disciples as followers of Jesus, we witness that Bartimaeus too begins to follow Jesus after he is healed.

We must be willing to ask specifically for healing in certain areas of our lives. Jesus knew Bartimaeus was blind and yet he still asked him, "What do you want me to do for you?" This is for Bartimaeus's sake, not his own. For our sakes, we need to tell Jesus how he can heal us. James 4:2 says, "You do not have, because you do not ask." We must state to him and to ourselves what we want him to do in our lives.

Finally, while our wounds can be incredibly painful, God uses them to strengthen our relationship with him. They give us opportunities to cry out to him. The work he does with our wounds can cause us to follow him more closely.

HOW TO BE HEALED

Jesus wants to heal us. Sometimes healing happens all at once. Other times, it takes place gradually, over years. Sometimes it doesn't happen at all, as in the case of St. Paul (2 Cor 12:7–10). The most important thing to remember is that no matter what happens with your suffering, God wants to bring good out of it. He wants to use it to bring you closer to him.

There are many ways to pursue healing. We can ask others to pray for us. We can call on the Holy Spirit to bring restoration to our lives. We can participate in the Church's sacraments, especially the Sacraments of Healing, such as Confession. We can also seek out medical and professional help. There's no shame in using a counselor to help you with whatever obstacle you face. Just make sure you find a good Catholic counselor who aligns the healing process to your faith.

As we seek out an identity in Jesus and healing of our wounds, tomorrow we will look at the attachments that keep us from a deeper relationship with him.

REFLECTION

The words of Bartimaeus, this bold blind beggar, have become one of the most uttered prayers in the history of Christianity. Out of the Eastern Orthodox faith there arose a tradition of repeating the words, "Jesus, Son of David, have mercy on me, a sinner," or some version of them. Dubbed "the Jesus Prayer," Bartimaeus's words help us to contemplate our own wounds and God's merciful healing. Take some time today to try the prayer yourself.

DAY 6—ATTACHMENTS

In the Gospel of Mark, Jesus has a profound encounter with a person often called the "rich young man" (10:17–22). The man approaches Jesus and kneels before him to ask a burning question, "Good Teacher, what must I do to inherit eternal life?" (v. 17).

Jesus responds by telling him to follow the commandments. The young man replies, "Teacher, all these I have observed from my youth." Jesus looks at him with love and says, "Go, sell what you have, and give to the poor, and you will have treasure in heaven; and come, follow me." The young man then becomes very sad, and he departs with sorrow. The text tells us the reason: "for he had great possessions."

Here we have a young man who respects Jesus. He is willing to follow all the commandments. He wants to gain eternal life. Yet even when Jesus tells him the two magic words that every Jewish boy wants to hear—*Lek Hackeri*, or "Come, follow me"— he is still unable to become Jesus' disciple. In fact, he is saddened by the awareness that he can't follow our Lord.

What stops him? He's attached to his possessions. I believe Jesus specifically asks the young man to give up his wealth because he knows that this is what the young man is attached to. Jesus has a simple principle: we can't be attached to this world *and* follow him.

Throughout the gospels, Jesus lets his followers know that they can't love anything more than him. If they love mother or father, sister or brother, or even their own lives more than him, they aren't worthy to be his disciples (Mt 10:37–38, Lk 14:26–27).

When we encounter Jesus, he calls us to something more. But we can't embrace him if we are holding on to other things. Peter, Andrew, James, and John can't follow Jesus if they cling to their nets. Matthew can't follow Jesus if he holds on to making money as a tax collector. Bartimeaus can't be healed and follow Jesus if he doesn't throw off his mantle.

Have you experienced this before? You know what Jesus wants you to do. You see the good Jesus wants done. And yet you make some excuse that holds you back. There's a sin or hesitation or selfishness that limits your freedom and your ability to say yes to the Lord. This attachment to other things instead of God is actually the root of all sin. The *Catechism* identifies sin as a "failure in genuine love for God and neighbor caused by a perverse *attachment* to certain goods" (*CCC* 1849, emphasis added). So how do we identify what we are attached to?

IDENTIFYING OUR ATTACHMENTS

There are three simple tests to identify your attachments:

1. *Consider how you spend your time.* Look closely at your daily life. What do you make time for? Time is one of our most valuable treasures, and I'm reminded of a verse in St. Matthew, "For where your treasure is, there will your heart be also" (6:21). Where is your heart when it comes to prayer and time with God? It's so easy to say that we are busy and can't find time to pray. But often when we look at our schedules, we are amazed at the things we find time for. Why? It's because we are attached to these things and value them. Try checking your web history or track the amount of time you spend on social media. This practice can be very convicting for me about what I truly value and spend time on.

2. *Identify what distracts you from prayer.* The *Catechism* tells us a deep truth regarding the relationship between prayer

and distraction: "The habitual difficulty in prayer is *distraction* . . . for a distraction reveals to us *what we are attached to*" (*CCC* 2729, emphasis added). Reading this paragraph from the *Catechism* can feel pretty defeating—apparently, I'm attached to a lot of things! But at the same time, it's good to know what I'm attached to.

3. *Begin to look at everything in your life.* In 2014, Marie Kondo came out with a book titled *The Life-Changing Magic of Tidying Up: The Japanese Art of Decluttering and Organizing.* This book on a seemingly obscure topic quickly became an international bestseller. Before long, multiple people, without my prompting, told me about this book and what they discovered. From my conversations with them (and a little research), I learned that Kondo recommends one main method for cleaning up. First, you gather things together from one area of the house. Then you lift up each one and ask, "Does this bring me joy?" The items that bring you the most joy go in the keep pile. The ones that don't bring much joy are thanked for their service and put in a pile to give away. [6]

I think Christians need to declutter too, but with a different question. We need to examine each thing in our life and ask, "Does this help me follow Jesus?" We should pick up our phone and our computer, look at our apps and favorite websites, and ask, "Do these things help me follow Jesus?" We should think about the TV shows and movies we watch and ask, "Do these help me follow Jesus?" Ladies, some of you need to pick up your boyfriends and, with their legs dangling in the air, ask, "Do you help me follow Jesus?" And if not, you should thank them for their service, put them aside, and let someone else date them. Boyfriends should do this too; in fact, we all need to ask this question with all of our relationships (but don't really pick up anyone). We can't embrace Jesus if we are holding on to other things. We can't follow him if we are staying behind occupied by lesser goods. We can't be his disciples while we love something else more than him.

OUR ATTACHMENTS ARE OPPORTUNITIES

The good thing about attachments is that they give us an opportunity to encounter Jesus. The *Catechism* says that the humble awareness of our attachments "should awaken our preferential love for him and lead us resolutely to offer him our heart to be purified" (*CCC* 2729). He wants to meet me, and he wants to meet you in these areas. When we face our attachments, we have the unique opportunity to say yes to Jesus. Each time we confront our attachments, he offers us the chance to say, "I love you more than these other things in my life." He wants to use these attachments to bring us closer to him. When we encounter our attachments, we have the opportunity to encounter Jesus. Slowly but surely, you will be able to say yes to him.

While the rich young man in the Gospel of Mark couldn't follow Jesus, another rich young man hundreds of years later did. Tomorrow we will look at how this passage transformed his life and how his example helped one great saint overcome the attachment that kept him from following Jesus.

REFLECTION

There's no better time than now to write down your attachments. Maybe as you went through this chapter, some came to mind. As you write down the things you find hard to let go of, talk to God and ask him what makes you so attached to these things. What is at the root of your love of them instead of God? Perhaps you'll discover new attachments while you are distracted in prayer. Throughout the next week, take the time to truly look at the things in your life and ask yourself, "Do these things help me follow Jesus?"

DAY 7—PHILIP

During this past week, we have looked at a number of examples of Jesus calling his disciples and understanding what that means. I want to add one more narrative for you to think about. It is the calling of two of Jesus' disciples that is only found in the Gospel of John.

> The next day Jesus decided to go to Galilee. And he found Philip and said to him, "Follow me." Now Philip was from Bethsaida, the city of Andrew and Peter. Philip found Nathanael, and said to him, "We have found him of whom Moses in the law and also the prophets wrote, Jesus of Nazareth, the son of Joseph." Nathanael said to him, "Can anything good come out of Nazareth?" Philip said to him, "Come and see." Jesus saw Nathanael coming to him, and said of him, "Behold, an Israelite indeed, in whom is no guile!" Nathanael said to him, "How do you know me?" Jesus answered him, "Before Philip called you, when you were under the fig tree, I saw you." Nathanael answered him, "Rabbi, you are the Son of God! You are the King of Israel! (Jn 1:43–49)

There is so much in this short passage, and much of it sums up our first week and where the rest of this book is going.

First, Philip must have had a profound encounter with Jesus. Philip is so moved by Jesus that he is convinced in a short period of time that Jesus is the Messiah ("of whom Moses in the law and also the prophets wrote"). We get a deeper glimpse of Nathaniel's encounter with Jesus. Nathaniel is moved and mystified—"How do you know me?" Can you imagine what these encounters must have been like?

These are the types of experiences that we've looked at in this first week. Each of our encounters with Jesus are so unique and, at the same time, they often cause the same effect—we are moved to want more. We are compelled to spend more time with Jesus and to learn more about him. This is exactly what we find with Philip and Nathaniel in this passage.

The encounter leads to the second stage, where we "come and see" and begin to follow Jesus. The disciples began to live with Jesus, and as we've learned about discipleship during this week, it is where they learned to be like Jesus. This is what the next week of this book is all about. After we've encountered him, what does it mean to become like Jesus. How do we emulate the Savior of the World?

Finally, Philip's reaction to Jesus sums up the final stage of this book—what we will look at in weeks three through five. After encountering Jesus and spending time with him, Philip tells his friend Nathaniel that he's found the Messiah. Philip didn't need a training course or book on evangelization to tell those he loved the good news that he's learned. While courses and books (like this one!) can be helpful, evangelization is best done naturally from our own encounters with Jesus. Our ability to encounter Jesus is vital to our ability to share him with others. When we stop encountering him, our witness grows cold and ineffective. However, when we encounter Jesus, we become a fire that people feel wherever we go.

It's been said that evangelization is nothing more than one beggar telling another where to find bread. Recall a moment when you told a friend about something great that happened to you. It probably felt natural to share this experience with your friend because you had encountered something profound, life-changing, or meaningful. The same should be true when we think about sharing our faith with others. Rather than viewing our efforts to talk about Jesus as a burden or an obligation, our encounter with Jesus should make it impossible not to share him with others. Philip demonstrates this beautifully. While learning more about Jesus as we follow him can help our evangelization, we can also begin to share Jesus with others even after our very first encounter with him.

Encounters change everything. My hope is that you see your own life in the life of these first disciples. Just as they began to follow him more closely after their encounters with him, I'm going to invite you to follow Jesus more closely as we head into week two. We'll explore what Jesus meant when he said, "Follow me," and what it can mean for you today.

REFLECTION

This week has been all about encounter. Take some time to think and pray about how you have encountered Jesus through the chapters and meditations in this section. My prayer is that you have encountered Jesus this week in multiple ways and that these moments help you continue to encounter Jesus in your life and to want to follow him.

A huge part of encountering Jesus is telling others about him.

My challenge for you is to tell someone about an encounter you had with Jesus this week. Share with them what you've learned and how it's affecting your life.

WEEK 2—DISCIPLE

DAY 8—IMITATION

Last week we looked at *how* rabbis called disciples. Today I want to look at *what* rabbis called their disciples to do. In other words, what was Jesus asking of his disciples when he called them during his earthly ministry, and what is he asking us to do today?

COVERED IN THE DUST OF YOUR RABBI

When a student heard the words *Lek Hackeri* ("Come, follow me"), he left his family and his village and followed the rabbi wherever he went. The disciple was to watch and imitate the rabbi. If the rabbi prayed a certain way, then the disciple also prayed that way. If the rabbi told a certain parable, then the student learned to tell that parable. There are even funny stories about disciples hiding under the rabbi's bed to make sure they caught a glimpse of everything that the rabbi did. A blessing developed: "May you be covered in the dust of your rabbi." The hope was that the disciple would follow so closely behind the rabbi that the dust from the rabbi's sandals covered him.

The idea behind all of this imitation is that the disciple strives to become the rabbi. When the rabbi calls the disciple, he is saying in effect, "I think you can be like me. I think you can do what I do." This perspective gives us a deeper understanding of why the disciples dropped everything to follow Jesus. Jesus, a teacher they had probably heard during their time with John the Baptist, thought that somehow they could be like him. I'm sure that despite their doubts, they had to find out whether or not it was true.

IMITATION IN SCRIPTURE

In Matthew 10, the gospel writer tells us, "These twelve Jesus sent out, charging them, 'Go nowhere among the Gentiles, and enter no town of the Samaritans, but go rather to the lost sheep of the house of Israel. And preach as you go, saying, "The kingdom of heaven is at hand." Heal the sick, raise the dead, cleanse lepers, cast out demons'" (vv. 5–8).

If we read this in the context of the Gospel of Matthew, we notice that Jesus commands the Twelve to go out and do what he has just been doing. Jesus just preached, "The kingdom of heaven is at hand." Jesus just healed the sick, raised the dead, cleansed the lepers, and cast out demons. Jesus modeled for the apostles how to do his work, and now he sends them out to do the same.

In the Gospel of John, Jesus tells his disciples, "Truly, truly, I say to you, he who believes in me will also do the works that I do; and greater works than these will he do, because I go to the Father" (Jn 14:12). Scholars believe that one of the main purposes of the Acts of the Apostles was to show that the apostles *could do what Jesus did*. In Acts, Peter and Paul heal people of their sickness, exorcise demons, and even raise the dead—just as Jesus had.

OUR IMITATION

Can you remember who you tried to imitate as a kid? Maybe an athlete, a movie star, or an older brother or sister? As a kid, I was head over heels into baseball. In the summer, I typically watched the morning sports highlights show twice just to make sure I caught everything. When I tuned in and saw my favorite baseball players on TV, I scrutinized their every move. I watched how they hit or played defense, but I also noticed how they dressed and celebrated. I wanted to be like them in everything that they did.

As Christians, we are supposed to take this desire to imitate others and apply it to Jesus. Our fundamental calling is not to be "good people." We aren't simply called to do the right thing. We are called to be like Jesus himself—to *imitate* our Lord and our God. Like his first disciples, we need to watch him and follow close behind.

For some, this might sound extreme. How can *we* be like Jesus? But St. Ambrose states this concept powerfully: "[God] wills that his disciples possess a tremendous power: that his lowly servants accomplish in his name all that he did [on earth]" (*CCC* 983).

Being like Jesus is what the second week of this book is all about. How do we follow him closely so that we can learn to be just like him? What advice does Jesus himself give for what it takes to be his disciple? In other words, how do we need to think and act differently to be his disciples?

While there are many possible lessons on what it means to be a disciple, I picked out a handful of powerful examples from Jesus' advice to his first disciples to help us understand how we can be better disciples of him today. Tomorrow we will look at one of Jesus' most radical teachings.

REFLECTION

1. When you were a kid, who did you want to be like? What did you do to imitate that person?
2. What do you think is the hardest part of trying to be like Jesus? What fears and hesitations arise when you contemplate doing this?

3. Do you already have something in mind that needs to change in your life? Take it to prayer each day this week.

DAY 9—BEATITUDES

At the beginning of his ministry, Jesus quickly rose in popularity. After calling his disciples, he traveled throughout his home region of Galilee, the northern and more remote part of Israel. There he announces that the kingdom of heaven is at hand as he teaches in Galilean synagogues and heals diseases and infirmities among the people. His fame spreads, and great crowds follow him as he heals many who are sick (Mt 4:17–24).

What comes next is perhaps Jesus' most popular teaching: the Sermon on the Mount, which includes the Beatitudes. To properly understand the Beatitudes, we have to first understand the context surrounding Jesus' ministry.

MESSIANIC CONTEXT

During the time of Jesus, the Jewish people were under Roman occupation. Since the destruction of their kingdom, the Babylonians, Persians, Greeks, and now Romans had all ruled over the Jews. The Romans oppressed the Jews and levied incredibly high taxes on them. At times, the people had to decide between paying their tithe to the Temple and paying the Romans. If they did both, they couldn't survive. The Jews believed that a messiah or new king would restore their kingdom and rule over Israel once again.

A part of this belief was that the messiah would overthrow the Jewish occupiers by violent force. Throughout the years, others had claimed to be the messiah and had rallied military campaigns in the backcountry of Galilee (we'll learn more about this philosophy in week 3 of this book). As people hear Jesus proclaiming that the kingdom of God is at hand and see him perform miracles just as the messiah was prophesied to perform, they wait in expectation for the revolution that Jesus will bring. All of this provides the backdrop to the Sermon on the Mount.

BLESSED ARE THEY

The Sermon on the Mount begins, "Seeing the crowds, [Jesus] went up on the mountain, and when he sat down his disciples came to him. And he opened his mouth and taught them" (Mt 5:1–2). Each of these details is important. In the Old Testament, Moses brought the Ten Commandments down the mountain to the people. Here, Jesus invites the crowds up the mountain to give them new commandments, eight Beatitudes.

> Blessed are the poor in spirit, for theirs is the kingdom of heaven.
> Blessed are those who mourn, for they shall be comforted.
> Blessed are the meek, for they shall inherit the earth.
> Blessed are those who hunger and thirst for righteousness, for they shall be satisfied.
> Blessed are the merciful, for they shall obtain mercy.
> Blessed are the pure in heart, for they shall see God.
> Blessed are the peacemakers, for they shall be called sons of God.
> Blessed are those who are persecuted for righteousness' sake, for theirs is the kingdom of heaven.
> Blessed are you when men revile you and persecute you and utter all kinds of evil against you falsely on my account. Rejoice and be glad, for your reward is great in heaven, for so men persecuted the prophets who were before you. (Mt 5:3–12)

HOW CAN THIS BE?

The word *beatitude* can be translated as "blessed," "happy," or "fortunate." But, in the context of Jesus' day, these so-called blessings proclaimed by Jesus would have been very countercultural. How fortunate are those who mourn and are persecuted? No, we want a messiah who will cause our enemies to mourn and to be persecuted. How fortunate are the meek and the poor in spirit? No, we want to stand joyful and proud over our foes.

The Jews of Jesus' day were surely dismayed by this teaching. How can this be? How can our long-awaited Messiah say something so different from what we expect? So different from what we believe should happen?

The *Catechism* explains that the Beatitudes "take up the promises made to the chosen people since Abraham. The Beatitudes fulfill the promises by ordering them no longer merely to the possession of a territory, but to the Kingdom of heaven" (*CCC* 1716). The people of God should not base their worth and happiness on the things of this world, the things that the nations hold dear. They should think with heaven in mind, not this earth.

This lesson for the Jews remains a great lesson for us as well. The Beatitudes are a reminder that, if we are truly dedicated to Jesus, our lives should look distinctly different from what the world expects. Just as Jesus called the Jews to think differently about how they saw the world and what brought them happiness, he calls us to do the same today. Ultimately, the Beatitudes teach us that "true happiness is not found in riches or well-being, in human fame or power, or in any human achievement—however beneficial it may be—such as science, technology, and art, or indeed in any creature, but in God alone, the source of every good and of all love" (*CCC* 1723).

The Beatitudes provide a moral standard for evaluating our own happiness. They run distinctly counter to what the world says will enrich us. It is so easy for the values of society to permeate our worldview. We can easily become consumed with the world's vision for happiness rather than our own. While we may give value to the principles in the Beatitudes, when push comes to shove, we often quickly run back to the perspective of the world.

LIGHT OF THE WORLD

Why does all of this matter? Jesus goes on in his Sermon on the Mount to explain the impact: "You are the light of the world. A city set on a hill cannot be hid. Nor do men light a lamp and put it under a bushel, but on a stand, and it gives light to all in the house. Let your light so shine before men, that they may see your good works and give glory to your Father who is in heaven" (Mt 5:14–16).

If we are going to be a light in this world, we have to look different than the darkness. We have to be people who stand out. We need to be people whom others look to and glorify God for what we do. We need to show the world that when we live with God's vision and perspective, we can transform our lives and our world. This is the type of people we must become, and the Beatitudes give us the vision we need to become a light to the world. Tomorrow, we will look at how we can live out this example through God's kingdom here on earth.

REFLECTION

Imagine being someone in Galilee who listened to Jesus. In your mind, you believed that Jesus was the Messiah, and as the Messiah, he would defeat all of your enemies through violence. Imagine your shock when Jesus proclaims the Beatitudes. Now, look at your own life today. What is your vision of happiness or fulfillment? How do the Beatitudes challenge this vision? How is Jesus calling you to see the world the way he does, and what can you do to put this vision into action this week?

DAY 10—KINGDOM

Many times when we read the Bible, we understand the individual stories but don't see the big picture. This is often the case with the Gospel of Matthew. Throughout his testimony about the life of Jesus, Matthew is unfolding a central message about Jesus step by step, if only we have the eyes to see.

In the opening verses of his gospel, Matthew gives Jesus' genealogy. Now, think of all the different ways that he could have opened the Greatest Story Ever Told! But Matthew has a good reason for starting this way. He wants to show how Jesus' line leads all the way back to King David and Abraham—just as it was prophesied about the Messiah.

Next we hear about Jesus' infancy. King Herod is disturbed because it appears that there is a new king of the Jews. He tells the wise men that he will pay this king homage, but instead he kills all the infants of Bethlehem as he seeks to destroy a potential rival to his throne.

The story then skips to the time of John the Baptist as he preaches to the masses—"Repent, for the kingdom of heaven is at hand" (Mt 3:2). When Jesus starts his ministry, his message sounds pretty similar to John the Baptist's—"[Jesus] went about all Galilee, teaching in their synagogues and preaching the gospel of the kingdom and healing every disease" (Mt 4:23).

Later in Matthew's gospel, Jesus sends the disciples out to preach on their own. What does he tell them to preach? The kingdom of heaven is at hand (Mt 10:7). In chapter 13, Jesus preaches the parables. What are they all about? The kingdom! In Matthew 16, Peter proclaims Jesus as the Messiah (the King!), the Son of the living God. What does Jesus do in response? He gives Peter the most important position in the kingdom by making him the head of the Church.

When we step back from the small stories to look at the bigger picture, we see that Matthew and Jesus have one overarching theme and message—the kingdom of God is at hand! (By the way, there are many more details in Matthew's gospel that reinforce this idea.)[1] The kingdom is the message that Matthew is so excited to share.

A DIFFERENT CULTURE

Kingdoms are not something that most of us are familiar with today, so Jesus' message is often not appreciated. A kingdom is not only a political entity but also a place with its own culture. If you've traveled to another part of the world or even a very different region within your own country, you know that in other cultures people speak, act, and think very differently than you do.

When Jesus preaches the Gospel of the kingdom, he is telling his listeners that there is a stark difference between their current way of speaking, acting, and thinking and what he proposes. He is bringing a paradigm shift, a whole new way of living, that is completely foreign to his own culture.

Rather than placing their identities in success or material possessions, Jesus wants people to live as sons and daughters of a Father who loves them so much that he is willing to die for them. Rather than valuing their ethnicity and nationality, Jesus wants them to see that their "neighbor" is every soul in this world. Rather than just seeking to build up their people, Jesus wants to renew their desire to be a light to the nations.

THE KINGDOM TODAY

So, where is this kingdom today? For Jesus, "the kingdom" and "the Church" are practically synonyms (Mt 16:18–19). The Church is how his kingdom continues here on earth, and if we want to be disciples of the King, we must be disciples in his kingdom.

The kingdom has radical implications for our lives. Here are three:

1. *We are invited to see the world as Jesus does, in a way that is revolutionary.* We bear a message that is fundamentally different than the way our world currently lives, and it takes guts to stand up and share it with others. When we live a kingdom lifestyle, our family, friends, and acquaintances look at us differently. Our views on sexuality, family size, morality, care for the poor, and other life decisions come under scrutiny. People who live as disciples of the kingdom are an enigma to their friends and relatives. Similar divisions occur between people of opposing political views, but disciples of the kingdom live not by their politics first but by their association with the kingdom. Members of the kingdom are called to be signs of contradiction to the world.

2. *We must be willing to work in and through his Church as we follow Jesus and seek to make followers of him.* Some parishes and dioceses don't always look like Jesus' kingdom on earth. Some bishops and priests don't always act like successors of the apostles. And many laity don't have much resemblance to the disciples of the early Church (okay, maybe they do with the ones in Paul's letter to the Corinthians). And yet our Catholic Church remains Jesus' kingdom here on earth. We are called to respect, submit to, and work with our hierarchy. We are called to love those in our parishes. We are called to build up Jesus' kingdom here on earth, even if it doesn't feel like it and even if we don't feel like it.

3. *We are called to announce this kingdom.* Out of love for others, we need to proclaim the kingdom to them by sharing the Good News and letting them know how it brings true joy and vitality to all areas of our lives. The kingdom of God here on earth should be a witness to what life looks like with Jesus. It should stand as a place of conversion for those who are fed up with the status quo and are looking for something more, something truly fulfilling.

Jesus' focus on the kingdom should give us pause. Where does his kingdom fit into our own lives, and do we value it as much as he does? If we seek to be his disciples, let us take some time to consider what it means to be disciples in his kingdom and how being a part of this kingdom influences our lives.

REFLECTION

1. What is distinctive about a kingdom or a culture? As a Catholic, do you have a real sense that our kingdom and thus culture should look very different than the world? How does this perspective affect how you live out your faith, particularly how you evangelize?
2. We can't love the King without also loving his kingdom. How does this view change how we respond to the authority of the Church? How does it change the way we see the teachings and rules of the Church?
3. What does it look like to announce the kingdom of God to others in our actions and words?

DAY 11—REVEALED

Paul Harvey, the radio broadcaster famous for his *The Rest of the Story* segments, told this story of Christmas.[2] There once was a man who "was not a scrooge, he was a kind, decent, mostly good man. Generous to his family, upright in his dealings with other men. But he just didn't believe all that incarnation stuff which the churches proclaim at Christmas Time. It just didn't make sense, and he was too honest to pretend otherwise. He just couldn't swallow the Jesus Story, about God coming to Earth as a man."

Not wanting to be a hypocrite, he told his family that he wouldn't be going to church this Christmas. As he sat at home, heavy snow began to fall. He began to hear a thudding sound, almost as if someone was throwing snowballs against his living room window. When he went to the front door to investigate, he found a flock of birds huddled miserably in the snow. They'd been caught in the storm and, in a desperate search for shelter, had tried to fly through his large landscape window.

He didn't want the birds to freeze to death, so he devised a plan to get them to go to the barn. He opened the barn doors and turned on the light. He put out food to entice them. He tried to catch them and shoo them, all to no avail. He realized that the birds were afraid of him and couldn't understand that he was trying to help them. He told himself, "If only I could be a bird . . . and mingle with them and speak their language. Then I could tell them not to be afraid. Then I could show them the way to the safe, warm barn. But I would have to be one of them so they could see, and hear, and understand."

It was at this moment that the church bells began to ring, and the man sank to his knees in the snow.

WE WANT TO SEE HIM

Jesus' coming to earth answers the heartfelt longing of humans to experience God face-to-face. We want to see, hear, and understand God himself, and through the Incarnation, Jesus gives us a way to know him. Many empathize with the woman in the gospels who had a hemorrhage for twelve years and was not healed. Despite her condition and being unclean, she reaches out to touch Jesus' cloak to be healed.

While we often chide doubting Thomas for questioning Jesus and lacking faith, there's a part of us that also wants to reach out and touch Jesus' side so that we too can be sure of the Resurrection. Jesus even speaks of us at that moment: "Blessed are those who have not seen and yet believe" (Jn 20:29). We wish we could live at the time of Jesus so that it would be easier to believe. What an amazing thing to see and experience God! Thankfully, we do have a very real way to experience God today, and it is through the Seven Sacraments of the Catholic Church.

JESUS HIMSELF

The *Catechism* tells us that "the sacraments are efficacious signs of grace, instituted by Christ and entrusted to the Church, by which divine life is dispensed to us" (*CCC* 1131). In other words, the sacraments are not only signs and symbols of God's grace, but they are vessels of grace as well. In the Eucharist, bread is a sign and symbol of the spiritual nourishment that we need, but it is actual spiritual nourishment as well. Jesus is present within—body, blood, soul, and divinity. In Baptism, water is a sign and symbol of the cleansing that our soul needs, but it actually cleans our souls as well.

Furthermore, it is Jesus *himself* who works through the sacraments: "[The sacraments] are *efficacious* because in them Christ himself is at work: it is he who baptizes, he who acts in his sacraments" (*CCC* 1127). In the sacraments, Jesus is the one we are experiencing. In the Sacrament of Reconciliation, the priest stands in place of Jesus as Jesus himself absolves us from our sins. In the Sacrament of Holy Communion, it is Jesus' body, blood, soul, and divinity that we consume.

Finally, the liturgy of the Catholic Church points back to God's saving events within history and makes them present to us. At the Last Supper, Jesus says, "Do this in remembrance of me" (Lk 22:19). As the *Catechism* explains, "The memorial is not merely the recollection of past events but the proclamation of the mighty works wrought by God for men. In the liturgical celebration of these events, *they become in a certain way present and real.* This is how Israel understands its liberation from Egypt: every time Passover is celebrated, the Exodus events are made present to the memory of believers so that they may conform their lives to them" (*CCC* 1363, emphasis added).

TANGIBLE

In sum, through the sacraments we can experience Jesus and become like him because we receive his actual grace, because Jesus himself works through the sacraments, and because in the liturgy, past events are re-presented for us to experience again. Through the sacraments we have a real and tangible way to experience and touch our Lord and Savior and to receive his grace. So, how do we practically do this? Here are three tips for living out the sacraments:

1. *Learn more about the sacraments.* We cannot love what we do not know. By learning more about the sacraments, we come to understand how they work and what they have to do with us. Start with the *Catechism of the Catholic Church* to learn more about the sacraments as a whole and about specific sacraments that interest you.

2. *Believe.* Faith is essential to an appreciation of the sacraments. It can be easy to go through the motions each week at Mass or when we go to Confession, but we have to remember that Jesus is truly present in these moments. Just like the woman with the hemorrhage, we must have a strong belief in Jesus as we reach out to touch him. When you are at Mass, take time to recognize and accept that Jesus is truly present. The same sacrifice offered at Calvary is offered for you in your parish each day.

3. *Participate frequently.* When we understand the sacraments, place our faith in Jesus' presence within them, and frequently participate in them, we begin to see how God's grace works in our lives in powerful ways. In the sacraments, we can open our hearts to God and ask him to be present with us. In our joys and our sorrows, we can invite Jesus into our lives in real and tangible ways.

REFLECTION

Through the sacraments, Jesus is truly with us. It is one thing to talk about the sacraments or to pray and meditate on them. But, in reality, the best thing is to experience them in a whole new way. Whether the information in this chapter is completely new to you or you've heard some of it before, find a way to more fully participate in the sacraments in the next two to three days. Go to Mass early and take time to reflect on the gift of the Eucharist. Go to adoration for an hour and just sit with our Lord. Overcome your fear of Reconciliation and confess your sins to the priest as if he were Jesus himself. The sacraments are tangible ways to become like Jesus. Find a way to know, love, and live like Jesus in these great mysteries.

DAY 12—PRAYER

Prayer is one of the most critical aspects of a Christian's life and also one of the most confusing. Christians have all sorts of different ways to pray (some of which you've already experienced in this book) and seemingly endless opinions of best practices. It is easy to be overwhelmed by the many options. As with other topics, we will turn to Jesus for guidance in this area.

IN SECRET

Earlier this week, we looked at the Beatitudes found in the Sermon on the Mount. Just after the Beatitudes, Jesus teaches his disciples about prayer: "But when you pray, go into your room and shut the door and pray to your Father who is in secret; and your Father who sees in secret will reward you" (Mt 6:6). Prayer appears to be an effective way to avoid the desires of this world precisely because prayer itself naturally leads us to escape from this world to share with God our perspective and to hear his.

The *Catechism* speaks beautifully of the heart and its relation to prayer: "The heart is the dwelling-place where I am, where I live; according to the Semitic or Biblical expression, the heart is the place 'to which I withdraw.' The heart is our hidden center, beyond the grasp of our reason and of others; only the Spirit of God can fathom the human heart and know it fully. The heart is the place of decision, deeper than our psychic drives. It is the place of truth, where we choose life or death. It is the place of encounter" (*CCC* 2563).

Prayer is how we seek to go out of this world and into a world all of our own and into a space where God can dwell. So, when we have gone to this place, how are we to pray? Jesus' disciples had the same question: "He was praying in a certain place, and when he ceased, one of his disciples said to him, 'Lord, teach us to pray, as John taught his disciples'" (Lk 11:1). Jesus responds to this request with one of the simplest yet most profound prayers of the Church: "Father, hallowed be thy name. Thy kingdom come. Give us each day our daily bread; and forgive us our sins, for we ourselves forgive every one who is indebted to us; and lead us not into temptation" (Lk 11:2–4).

This prayer is worth sitting with. Given that we often have this same question about prayer, it's important for us to carefully listen to and understand Jesus' response. Let's go through the prayer line by line to explore the depth of Jesus' rich and meaningful words here. As you'll see, the Our Father covers many of the themes we've already looked at in the first two weeks of this book.

Father, hallowed be thy name. The very start of the prayer reminds us of our identity in the Trinity, as we saw on day 4. God is Father, and as we take time to step out of this world, we recognize this identity more clearly. "Prayer is the living relationship of the children of God with their Father who is good beyond measure, with his Son Jesus Christ and with the Holy Spirit" (*CCC* 2565).

Thy kingdom come. During our Baptism, the priest baptizes us in the name of the Father, the Son, and the Holy Spirit. This is how we become members of God's kingdom, the Church. As members of this kingdom, we know that we need to live differently. As we saw on day 10, we can't continue in our old ways and with our old identities. In prayer, we have the opportunity to reflect on how we are bringing about this kingdom on earth as we examine our lives.

Give us each day our daily bread. This appeal for daily bread speaks both of our natural needs and of our need for a supernatural food, the Eucharist (as we saw yesterday). It is worth noting that to ask for our *daily* bread, we need to be praying *daily*. We need both natural and supernatural means to carry out God's work. In prayer, make requests to God for your needs, especially for the ones that allow you to live out your identity and to advance his kingdom.

Forgive us our sins, for we ourselves forgive every one who is indebted to us. The Church gives us the Sacrament of Reconciliation as a Sacrament of Healing. We are healed from our brokenness through forgiveness and by receiving God's grace in the sacraments. In turn, we can forgive others because he has forgiven us first.

. . . and lead us not into temptation. The *Catechism* tells us, "There is a certain usefulness to temptation. . . . We discover our evil inclinations and are obliged to give thanks for the goods that temptation has revealed to us" (Origen, quoted in *CCC* 2847). Temptation reveals our attachments, and as we saw, what distracts us in prayer is often what we are attached to. Rather than simply trying to avoid distractions, we can pray through our attachments and ask the Lord to free us of the things that keep us from him and to provide the healing that we need to live out our true identities.

METHOD OF PRAYER

Spiritual masters throughout the ages have recommended that we spend twenty to thirty minutes in meditative prayer each day (start with less and work your way up), picking the same place and time each day (before noon works best). While there are many methods of prayer, below I'll share four steps of a very common method that I've modified from the teachings of saints and Doctors of the Church.

Preparation. The saints often comment that preparation is the most important part of our conversation with the Lord. We calm our minds from distractions and remind ourselves that we are speaking to the God who loves us and listens when we call on him for help and guidance.

Consideration. Once we clear our minds and recognize our Lord's presence, we can turn to the material that we have chosen, whether scripture or some other spiritual reading. As we read, we ask the Lord what he wants to tell us through our experience with it.

Conversation. After we have thought about the scripture or spiritual text, we talk to God about our experience with it and have a general conversation, as with a friend. We might talk to him about what we are going through right now and ask for his help. We may apologize for the times we have failed in our relationship with him and others. We may thank and praise him for particular blessings that we are currently receiving. We may also intercede on behalf of others.

Conclusion. As our time of prayer draws to a close, we thank God for the time we have spent with him, and we ask him to show us how to take what we have learned through our daily meditation and utilize it in how we live our lives. Traditionally, the saints encourage us to take this step by making a resolution. Many find it helpful to record their resolutions in a notebook or prayer journal, and to return to their resolutions each day in prayer.

BE RESOLUTE

Prayer is essential to the Christian life—we must be resolute in keeping this appointment with our Lord. If you haven't been consistent in the past, start by praying just five to ten minutes each day. Once you establish the routine, you can increase the amount of time in prayer. We can't give what we don't have, and prayer continually renews our relationship with the Lord so that we can give of ourselves to others. Make it a vital part of your relationship with God and your daily routine.

REFLECTION

Perhaps the best way to reflect on today's lesson is to put prayer into practice. Using the Our Father as your material, walk through the four steps outlined above.

Preparation: Quiet yourself and get past the things that distract you. Remember that as a loving Father, God himself is present with you and wants to be with you.

Consideration: Read the Our Father slowly. What stands out to you? What is God trying to tell you?

Conversation: Talk to God about the Our Father and a particular part that you relate to. Talk to God like a friend, and feel free to speak to him about other things in your life and other prayer intentions you have.

Conclusion: Thank God for your time with him and make a resolution based on your experience in prayer.

DAY 13—MARGINALIZED

On a given weekday in downtown Denver, Colorado, you can find the Christ in the City missionaries on one of their street walks. Three to four times a week, they walk the same path through downtown, greeting their friends—the homeless men and women they serve. Anything that friends would do for one another, these missionaries and homeless do for each other. Missionaries become the poor's emergency contacts. They accompany their friends to their pregnancy appointments to view ultrasounds. Both the missionaries and homeless invest in one another, sharing their struggles and joys and becoming close.

They are with them through the good and the bad.

The Christ in the City missionaries are an inspiration to my family and many others in Denver and across the country.[3] They minister to the poor in a way that is authentic, practical, and a remarkable example to Catholics of how they can approach those in need.

They also invite others into their work. Once a month they welcome about 150 of their homeless friends and 100 volunteers to a picnic in the park, where the homeless and volunteers have conversations about life and build up their friendships as well.

PREFERENTIAL OPTION FOR THE POOR

The Catholic Church's love of the poor comes from a deep scriptural tradition. In Matthew 25, Jesus gives us a sober reflection on the Last Judgment. He recounts that the Son of Man will separate people into two groups, one on his right hand and the other on his left.

On the right are those who will inherit the kingdom because they've helped the poor. Except they haven't just helped the poor, they've helped Jesus himself. With some confusion, the righteous in the parable ask, "Lord, when did we see you hungry and feed you, or thirsty and give you drink? When did we see you a stranger and welcome you, or naked and clothe you? When did we see you ill or in prison, and visit you?" (vv. 37–39, NABRE). Jesus answers them, "Amen, I say to you, whatever you did for one of these least brothers of mine, you did for me" (v. 40, NABRE). In contrast, on the left are those who will not inherit the kingdom because they did not help the poor.

Jesus' logic in this passage is very clear. First, he identifies the poor in a profound way. He forces us to rethink how we view the poor because he equates the poor with himself. Whether we help or do not help the poor is whether we do or do not help Jesus.[4] Second, he connects our eternal status to our treatment of the poor. Referencing this passage, Archbishop Charles J. Chaput of Philadelphia has stated, "I've said many times over many years that if we ignore the poor, we will go to hell: literally."[5]

MORE THAN THE MATERIALLY POOR

When we think of the poor, we almost always picture someone as homeless or begging on the streets. But the Church has a greater vision when it comes to those in need. The *Catechism* states, "[Love of the poor] extends not only to material poverty but also to the many forms of cultural and religious poverty" (*CCC* 2444).

Because of this broad view of poverty, the Church identifies not only corporal works of mercy but spiritual works of mercy as well. In fact, those who work closely with the poor such as the Christ in the City missionaries recognize that even the materially poor aren't just looking for food and shelter. Many times they are desperate for friendship and spiritual help as well.

THE CORPORAL WORKS OF MERCY (BASED ON THE JUDGMENT OF THE NATIONS IN MATTHEW 25)

Feeding the hungry
Giving drink to the thirsty
Clothing the naked
Offering hospitality to the stranger
Caring for the sick
Visiting the imprisoned
Burying the dead

THE SPIRITUAL WORKS OF MERCY

Instructing the ignorant
Counseling the doubtful
Admonishing the sinner
Bearing wrongs patiently
Forgiving injuries willingly
Comforting the sorrowful
Praying for the living and the dead

As we look at the Church's teachings on the poor, for the first time or perhaps pondering them anew, we may wonder: What's behind all of this? Why is this the logic of God?

WHO IS HELPING WHOM?

To Christians, Jesus' words in Matthew 25 seem confusing at first. Does our salvation depend on our deeds and, in this case, specifically our deeds to the poor? While I won't attempt to wade into a theological conversation about salvation and the role of faith versus works, I do think that there is a deep underlying reason for our Lord's commands that speaks to the heart of our faith.

The duty to help the poor goes back well before Jesus' ministry. After the Israelites escape from Egypt, they are called to help the poor: "You shall not wrong a stranger or oppress him, for you were strangers in the land of Egypt" (Ex 22:21). This is just one of many verses that shed light on why it is so important to help the poor: when we are merciful to the poor, we remember God's mercy *to us*. The converse is true as well: if we aren't merciful to the poor, then we must not understand and accept God's mercy in our own lives. (God has the same logic for forgiveness as well. See Matthew 6:15.)

St. Augustine once said, "Man is a beggar before God."[6] In other words, *we* are not living in our true home here on earth. *We* are hungry for a different food to satisfy. *We* are in desperate need of mercy. *We* are desperate for friendship with God. The poor remind us of this reality, and helping *them* can transform how *we* experience God. It is one of the best ways that we can imitate Jesus and become like him.

HELPING THE POOR

How do we help the poor? The best answer is friendship. The missionaries at Christ in the City know how to become friends with the poor. Here are three quick tips from them on how we can live this out. While they apply more directly to those who experience material poverty, they help us to address spiritual poverty as well.

1. *Introduce yourself and ask the person's name.* Sometimes someone living on the street can go weeks without hearing their name. Just like any friendship, begin by meeting the person. They'd much rather be known and loved than to

receive a five-dollar bill. Shake their hand, say hello. Just to receive some type of touch in a world that often ignores and shuns them can go a long way.

2. *Meet their needs.* Instead of giving someone on the street money, give them something that meets their needs. If it is hot outside, offer them bottled water. If it is raining, give out dry socks. If it is cold, hand out a cup of coffee or gloves. Meeting their needs tells them that you thought of them as a friend would. Prepare and place blessing bags in your car to give out to the people you see.

3. *Pray for them.* Intercede on their behalf, just as you would do for a friend or for Jesus if you saw him on the street. Prayer helps us realize that ultimately God is in control and to be detached from the fruits of our work.

REFLECTION

Take a look at the spiritual and corporal works of mercy listed in this chapter. What's one corporal or spiritual work of mercy that you would like to grow in over the next two weeks?

DAY 14—SOWER

As we did at the end of last week, let's look at how what we've learned this week relates to evangelization and discipleship. In regard to evangelization, our ability to reach others is tied closely to our relationship with God and our pursuit of holiness. How do we know this? Well, like most things in this book, I'll let Jesus explain.

> "Listen! A sower went out to sow. And as he sowed, some seed fell along the path, and the birds came and devoured it. Other seed fell on rocky ground, where it had not much soil, and immediately it sprang up, since it had no depth of soil; and when the sun rose it was scorched, and since it had no root it withered away. Other seed fell among thorns and the thorns grew up and choked it, and it yielded no grain. And other seeds fell into good soil and brought forth grain, growing up and increasing and yielding thirtyfold and sixtyfold and a hundredfold." And he said, "He who has ears to hear, let him hear." (Mk 4:3–9)

CONFUSED DISCIPLES

Jesus knows his audience. He is talking to a crowd in the country, and he uses an agricultural example to explain his teaching. And yet the apostles, who were just chosen to follow Jesus in Mark 3, still don't get it. They give me hope for the many times I don't fully understand Jesus. Jesus tells his confused disciples, "Do you not understand this parable? How then will you understand all

62

the parables?" (Mk 4:13). Apparently there's some downside to being God and trying to talk to human beings who don't know everything (#DeityProblems). So, Jesus decides to share the parable's meaning, which is a great benefit to his early disciples and us today.

> The sower sows the word. And these are the ones along the path, where the word is sown; when they hear, Satan immediately comes and takes away the word which is sown in them. And these in like manner are the ones sown upon rocky ground, who, when they hear the word, immediately receive it with joy; and they have no root in themselves, but endure for a while; then, when tribulation or persecution arises on account of the word, immediately they fall away. And others are the ones sown among thorns; they are those who hear the word, but the cares of the world, and the delight in riches, and the desire for other things, enter in and choke the word, and it proves unfruitful. But those that were sown upon the good soil are the ones who hear the word and accept it and bear fruit, thirtyfold and sixtyfold and a hundredfold. (Mk 4:14–20)

FRUITFUL SOIL

Jesus illustrates that not all people who accept the faith have the same reaction to it. In fact, some have the Word right in front of them but aren't able to receive it.

Some receive the Word of God, but because they don't have roots, their faith withers away. Most of us have probably witnessed this in the life of someone we know. At one point they believed in God and lived out their faith, but ultimately their faith didn't endure. Roots provide stability to plants. They allow a plant to stay firmly in place amidst strong winds. Also, when a plant lacks an immediate water source, its roots stretch down into the soil to find nourishment. In our faith lives, roots are necessary to overcome challenges, tribulations, and persecution. They give our faith stability and nourishment in these moments. When we pursue holiness with our Lord, he nurtures and strengthens the roots necessary to sustain our faith.

Next, there are those who don't lose the faith but aren't fruitful. Jesus says that "the cares of the world, and the delight in riches, and the desire for other things, enter in and choke the word." When flowers and thorns battle it out, thorns almost always win. The same is true with our spiritual lives. If we allow other things to compete with our devotion to God, even potentially good desires, our faith will not be fruitful.

How many Catholics do you know who have heard the Word but aren't fruitful? Perhaps they lack a transformative experience with the Word of God. Or maybe they hear the Word of God and accept it, but just don't know how to tell others. But many times, the pleasures of this life sequester God to only *a part* of their lives (maybe just for an hour on Sunday) instead of *the center* of their lives. Because of these competing interests, despite hearing the Word, they aren't fruitful.

Pope Paul VI said, "The person who has been evangelized goes on to evangelize others. Here lies *the test of truth*, the touchstone of evangelization: *it is unthinkable* that a person should accept the Word and give himself to the kingdom without becoming a person who bears witness to it and proclaims it in his turn" (*Evangelii Nuntiandi*, 24, emphasis added). For Paul VI, evangelization is the test of whether we have the faith or not. Many times people don't share the faith because they, in fact, don't have it.

BEAR FRUIT

Jesus closes the parable of the sower by giving us hope: "But those that were sown upon the good soil are the ones who hear the word and accept it and bear fruit, thirtyfold and sixtyfold

and a hundredfold." Look at what happens when we accept the
Word of God in our lives! Look at what happens when we pre-
vent the things of this world from competing with our love of
Jesus! Thirty-, sixty-, and a hundredfold!

If we try to evangelize without deepening our relationship
with Jesus, we risk becoming fruitless, or even worse, we can
lose our faith. We must be grounded in him. We must grow deep
roots in our Lord.

This week has been all about doing just that. Take what
you've learned this week and incorporate it into your own life.

REFLECTION

Think about this past week. What did you learn about imitat-
ing Jesus? If you are going to be fruitful (thirty-, sixty-, or even
a hundredfold), what does your life have to look like? Often
we think we need to have amazing gifts or talents or that we
have to change our lives all at once. But usually, our imitation of
Jesus and our fruitfulness come by taking small steps in the right
direction. What have you already started to put into practice?
What do you still want to put into practice? Continue along this
path and see where the Lord leads you.

WEEK 3—VISION

DAY 15—FADED

Over the last two weeks, we've looked at how to encounter Jesus and how to be his disciple. These are two of the essential lessons we can learn as followers of Jesus, and they provide a strong foundation for what we will discuss over the next three weeks. As we saw in the last chapter, our ability to be Jesus' disciples allows us to be fruitful. This week we will focus on why we need to evangelize—to not only be a disciple of Jesus but also to make disciples of others. While this week might be very intense, stick with it! I promise it will be worth it!

We'll start by once again focusing squarely on Jesus—his words, his actions, and his logic. I want to start this process by exploring the world of Jesus, and there are few better ways to do that than delving into one of the richest (and least-known) narratives in the entire Old Testament, found in 1 and 2 Maccabees.

These two books give two accounts of the same events that unfolded less than 150 years before the time of Jesus Christ. The Jewish holiday of Hanukkah celebrates the events of this period. Maccabees tells the story of the Jewish people trying to preserve their religion and culture under an intense and hostile takeover by the Greek emperor Antiochus IV Epiphanes. Keep in mind that the Jews were no strangers to being ruled by foreign powers. But, up until this point, the foreign nations who ruled over them, the Greeks included, did not interfere much in their religion and culture. Antiochus IV Epiphanes changed all of this, and the book of 1 Maccabees opens with a gruesome account of what occurs during his siege of Jerusalem. The Greeks overran the city and ransacked the Temple, taking all of its gold and other valuables (1 Mc 1:20–24). They killed any Jews who tried to remain faithful to their covenant with the Lord. They forced men and women to make sacrifices to pagan gods (1 Mc 2:15). They slaughtered anyone with the scriptures in their possession, and any child found circumcised was hung from its mother's neck (1 Mc 1:60–61).

THE BEAUTY OF THE WOMEN FADED

Not only do we witness the Greeks' destruction of Jerusalem, but we also see how the Jews reacted to this onslaught.

> In those days lawless men came forth from Israel, and misled many, saying, "Let us go and make a covenant with the Gentiles round about us, for since we separated from them many evils have come upon us." This proposal pleased them, and some of the people eagerly went to the king. He authorized them to observe the ordinances of the Gentiles. So they built a gymnasium in Jerusalem, according to Gentile custom, and removed the marks of circumcision, and abandoned the holy covenant. They joined with the Gentiles and sold themselves to do evil. (1 Mc 1:11–15)

Some of the Jews were willing to join forces with the Greeks and abandon their covenant with God. One of the practical ways that the Jews rejected their faith was by building a gymnasium. To a modern person, the idea of having a gym and working out seems pretty innocent. But for the Greeks, the gymnasium was central to the social life of their culture and their spirituality. The Greeks believed that the physical appearance of a person reflected the beauty of the spirit. The more perfect the body, the more perfect the soul. In Greek gymnasiums, males worked out in the nude to show off their physicality (and spirituality, apparently) to others.

For the Jews, this whole nudity and perfection thing was a problem if they were to fit into Greek culture. The mark of their faith and covenant with God was circumcision, which was considered a physical imperfection to the Greeks. Some Jews wanted to assimilate into the Greek culture so much that they went through a painful surgery to reverse their circumcision.

The author of 1 Maccabees offers a poetic reaction to the suffering that Antiochus and his Jewish followers dealt to faithful Jews: "Israel mourned deeply in every community, rulers and elders groaned, maidens and young men became faint, the beauty of the women faded. Every bridegroom took up the lament; she who sat in the bridal chamber was mourning. Even the land shook for its inhabitants, and all the house of Jacob was clothed with shame" (1 Mc 1:25–28).

There are few lines in the Bible that strike me as much as "the beauty of the women faded." What a great sign of despair! The beauty of the world dissolves amid the ongoing catastrophe. The joy of marriage is squelched. The tragedy of the situation causes brides and grooms to mourn: Who would want to get married and raise children at a time such as this?

OUR CULTURE TODAY

When I read scripture, I try to remind myself that these were real people. They had jobs and families. They had hopes and dreams. They had fears and doubts. They were just like us. As I think and pray with the pages of Maccabees, I ask myself: What would I do in this situation? What would I do if I had that kind of pressure to give up my faith? How would I respond if I saw many of my family members and friends give in to this pressure? What would I do in the face of this violence and oppression?

While the story of Maccabees may sound strange at first, we come to realize that our culture today is not all that different. The story of Maccabees provides key examples to us as everyday disciples in a post-Christian world. We don't face a dictator or emperor who attempts to wipe out our culture and faith through violence, but our secular Western culture does seek to eliminate our belief system. In the words of Pope Benedict XVI, "We are moving toward a dictatorship of relativism which does not recognize anything as for certain and which has as its highest goal one's own ego and one's own desires."[1] The results have been disastrous for our world and our Church. Just as in the time of Maccabees, our religious freedom is waning. Just as in the time of Maccabees, people (and in particular children in the womb) are being eliminated in the name of choice. The dictatorship of relativism has a high price for us today.

Amid the onslaught of moral relativism and the rejection of objective truth, we've all witnessed the reaction of our own people. While we don't see members of our Church reversing their circumcision, we do see them abandoning the sign of the new covenant—their Baptism. Repeatedly, we see Catholics leave the Church, even some who learned the faith through Catholic schooling or from solid Catholic parents. Lukewarm and mediocre faith seems to be the norm as Catholics make any and every excuse to discard their covenants with God and basic Christian morality to pursue the goods of this world. We may prefer to ignore the great exodus that is happening on a daily basis in our Church, but the reality is astounding and overwhelming when we face it.

In addition, just like the Jews in the story of Maccabees, many former Catholics, or so-called Catholics who have given up their faith, work to undermine the Church, to weaken its influence, and to bring division and discord. How many politicians and celebrities claim to be Catholic and at the same time question or openly defy Church teaching? How many Church leaders, religious and lay alike, give scandal as they abandon the teachings of the Church for the ways of the world?

Just like the Jews in the story of Maccabees, we too have to ask: What will our reaction be? How should we live as everyday disciples in this post-Christian world?

The answer to this question is difficult, complex, and at times subjective, but I believe the source of our answers is pretty straightforward. What if we asked how Jesus would respond to the current crisis? What would he do if he lived today? Jesus lived in an age much like Maccabees and in many ways a society that is looking more and more like our own. Tomorrow we will look at how Jesus reacted to a hostile takeover in his day and what this might mean for us today.

REFLECTION

1. As you take in the Maccabees narrative and the situation that the Jews found themselves in, how do you think you'd react to the pressure to give up your faith, to your friends and family abandoning the faith, and to the violence at that time?
2. As a Church, what is our answer to how we should live in this post-Christian culture?
3. How do you think Jesus would react to this situation? What would he do?

DAY 16—JESUS

After the Greeks, the Romans ruled over the Jews. During this time, the Jewish historian Josepheus identified four distinct groups that each had a different reaction to the Roman occupation.[2] These groups set the context for many of Jesus' words and actions and, in turn, help us learn how to respond to our current situation. Let's look at all four groups: Essenes, Zealots, Sadducees, and Pharisees.

FOUR GROUPS

THE ESSENES

The Essenes believed that the Jewish authorities, through their cooperation with foreign invaders, had corrupted both the holy city of Jerusalem and its Temple. They moved out of the city and lived like monks. They believed that their holiness and strict following of the Law would provoke God to send the Messiah they so desperately needed to free them from the foreign influence that had overtaken the Jewish culture. Out of the four groups, the Essenes are the only ones who have no recorded interactions with Jesus.

THE ZEALOTS

The Zealots would not tolerate the pagan rule of their land or their Temple and were willing to use force to take back what was rightfully theirs. As we mentioned in the section on the

Beatitudes, most Jews of Jesus' era thought the messiah would lead a violent revolution, defeating their pagan occupiers and reestablishing a Jewish king as the leader of the people. The Zealots were eager to make this happen, with or without a messiah. We see evidence of the Zealots even within Jesus' apostles—Simon the Zealot (Acts 1:13).

THE SADDUCEES

In direct contrast to the first two groups, the Sadducees seemingly welcomed their Roman overlords with open arms. They were seen as Jewish elitists who wanted to maintain the priestly caste and likewise the power that came with it. They did not believe in the afterlife, which is why they were *sad*, you see. (I couldn't help myself. This is the only pun in the book, I promise.) In the Gospels, they pose a question to Jesus on eternal life, attempting to trap him (Mt 22). I'll let you read the story on your own, but spoiler alert: Jesus wins the debate.

The Sadducees were one of two parties to make up the Sanhedrin, a Supreme Court–like body of Jewish leaders. Jesus goes before the Sanhedrin and is condemned to die before being taken to Pontius Pilot (Lk 22:66–71). In the Acts of the Apostles, John and Peter appear before the Sanhedrin as well (Acts 4:1–22).

THE PHARISEES

Our last group, the other group who made up the Sanhedrin, were the Pharisees, a term that means "pure" or "separated." The Pharisees were perhaps the most important group of ancient Jews. The Pharisees were known as *rabbis*, a title that is still used for teachers of Judaism today, and their philosophy forms much of modern Judaism. (Remember we studied how they played a part in the Jewish education system on day 2.) This group of thousands of teachers across Israel (Josephus notes that around six thousand refused to swear an oath to Caesar during the reign of Herod the Great)[3] believed that by upholding the Torah and living out the faith to the letter of the Law, they would bring about the coming of the messiah. This is why they went to great lengths to promote holiness and shun sin in their communities. They wanted to make sure that they held on to their identity as a people. Upholding laws that defined them as Jews was extremely important (ceremonial handwashing, who they ate with, circumcision, the Sabbath, and so on).

WHAT GROUP ARE YOU IN?

Each one of these groups gives us a glimpse of how someone might react to being overtaken by a foreign power. One could seek to escape the world by removing themselves from it like the Essenes. One could fight back against the culture with violence like the Zealots. One could embrace the culture for the sake of preservation and power like the Sadducees. Or one could live in the culture but strive for holiness and protect their identity like the Pharisees. While first-century Judaism carries unique characteristics, many of which are different from those of our own world, I believe that these four types of reactions represent the most immediate options we have in our culture as well.

Think about how many Catholics react to our culture today. Some are like Essenes: In response to the challenges in our culture, they run for the hills. They seek to remove themselves from the world, hoping that one day it will get better. Perhaps their pursuit of holiness outside of the world will eventually renew it.

Some are like Zealots. Modern Catholics aren't prone to using physical violence to defend the faith, but many defend the faith as if it's a war. They seek vindication, forgetting charity and the work required to win a soul. They strive to win political battles, assuming that the faith can be won through elections and the powers of this world.

Others are like Sadducees—people who claim to be Catholic but are willing to give up certain doctrines and practices to fit into the culture. They desire to be well respected in the world and seek its praise rather than witness to a faith that might not be popular or well received. They use their power to subvert the Church and try to get it to change its beliefs to fit in.

Some are like Pharisees: Catholics who seek holiness in the world but often remain separated from the culture. They know all the rules of Catholicism and shun those who live outside of these rules. They want to keep their Catholic identity at all costs, even if it means not evangelizing others.

You see, the four groups in Jesus' day are also strong in ours. Each one of them harms Jesus' mission in a different way, and if we want to see our Church become one that evangelizes, we have to help people overcome their misperceptions of what the Church is supposed to be. The key mistake in each of our groups today—which was also the key mistake for each Jewish group—is misunderstanding our identity. To know our identity, we have to understand God's original plan for the salvation of the world.

REFLECTION

1. Why do you think that Jesus came as a person who most resembles a Pharisee? Why not the other three groups?
2. Which group of Jews do you most identify with (Essenes, Zealots, Sadducees, Pharisees)?
3. How does this perspective change the way that you think about our culture and live within it?

DAY 17—SALVATION

This week we are identifying the reasons to evangelize. To start this journey, we focused on the culture that Jesus lived in through the story of Maccabees and the four prominent groups of Jews who reacted to their Roman occupiers. The problem with their reactions was a misunderstanding of their identity as a people of God. To comprehend this identity, we need to go back to the beginning of God's covenant with the Jews and the story of Abram/Abraham found in Genesis 12. Then we will see how Jesus seeks to restore who God's people were originally called to be.

THREE PROMISES, THREE COVENANTS

The story of the Jewish people really starts with three crucial verses in Genesis 12: "Now the LORD said to Abram, 'Go from your country and your kindred and your father's house to the land that I will show you. And I will make of you a great nation, and I will bless you, and make your name great, so that you will be a blessing. I will bless those who bless you, and him who curses you I will curse; and by you all the families of the earth shall bless themselves'" (vv. 1–3). These three verses are perhaps the most important in the Old Testament because they describe three promises that will play a pivotal role in the life of Abraham and the story of God's people. For Abram, each promise is raised to a covenant at a different time in his life. For the story of God's people, the fulfillment of these covenants provides an outline for the rest of scripture.

The first promise is about "the land that I will show you," a location that would later be known as the Promised Land. This covenant is fulfilled by Moses and Joshua when they lead the people out of Egypt and into the Promised Land after forty years of wandering in the desert.

The second promise is about having a great nation and a great name. When God promises that he will make Abram's name great, this is a reference to kingship. This covenant is fulfilled when David becomes the king of Israel.

The third promise is the most important one for understanding the identity of God's people and our own role today. Let's take some time to really grasp what God was telling Abraham and how this promise would be fulfilled.

A FUTURE SACRIFICE

The third promise is, "and by you all the families of the earth shall bless themselves." Just because God chose Abram and his descendants to be his people doesn't mean that he forgot the rest of humanity. In fact, God planned that his chosen people would remain blameless and follow him—and would also be a light to the rest of the world. The story of Abram shows how this promise was dramatically fulfilled.

In Genesis 22, Abram (now known as Abraham) is asked to kill his only son, Isaac. After the angel stops Abraham from killing his son, the Lord provides a ram to take Isaac's place. The sacrifice of the ram symbolizes an even larger promise that God is making. Following this episode, the author of Genesis states, "Abraham called the name of that place The LORD will provide; as it is said to this day, 'On the mount of the LORD it shall be provided'" (22:14).

It was still said in the author's day that "the Lord *will* provide," or in Hebrew, *Yahweh Yireh*. What was the point of God providing something or someone in the future? The text makes

clear that this future sacrifice was to fulfill the third promise—
that Abraham's descendants would bless all nations: "By myself
I have sworn, says the LORD, because you have done this . . .
and by your descendants shall all the nations of the earth bless
themselves" (Gn 22:16, 18).

The Jews believed so much in this promise that they changed
the name of the city closest to this mountain when they came
into the Promised Land. The city of Salem would now be called
Jeru-salem, with the word *Yireh* being placed at the beginning
of the word *Salem*. The city of Jerusalem stood as a constant
reminder that the Lord would provide a sacrifice there that
would allow the Jewish people to bless all the nations.

AN UNRAVELING KINGDOM

After the fulfillment of the first covenant with the Promised
Land under Moses and Joshua and the fulfillment of the second covenant of kingship under David, the Israelites start to fall
apart. The twelve tribes divide into two kingdoms, the north (ten
northern tribes called Israel) and the south (the tribes of Judah
and Benjamin, commonly known as the Jews). Both Israel and
the Jews are conquered, enslaved, and taken into exile. While
Judah eventually returns from Babylon, the ten northern tribes
intermarry and never return.

During this time of exile and captivity, the prophets remind
the people of God's promises. For instance, Isaiah prophesizes
about a messiah who will come and restore the Jewish people.
This suffering servant will be "as a light to the nations, that my
salvation may reach to the end of the earth" (Is 49:6). The proph-
et reminds his people that even though they are in captivity
and it is difficult to see it now, God will remain faithful to his
promises. God will still bless all the nations of the earth through
their descendants.

JESUS CHRIST, THIRD COVENANT SUPERSTAR

As you can imagine, it was hard for the Jewish people to maintain belief in this narrative over time. While they knew the scriptures well, there had to be a sense that perhaps it was all too good to be true. On a very human level, it would be easier to take steps to protect oneself. In light of all of this background, the four types of reactions that we saw yesterday make a lot of sense. Instead of trusting in God's promise, some decided to run away (Essenes), to fight other nations as their enemies (Zealots), to join forces with their enemies (Sadducees), or to strive for holiness and shun those who didn't follow the Law (Pharisees).

And yet Jesus comes to make all things new. Jesus comes to redeem what was lost. To restore what has failed. To breathe life into his people once again. He is the descendant of Abraham and David whom God uses to bless the nations. As you can guess, Jesus is ultimately the fulfillment of God's third covenant. In St. John the Baptist's words, "Behold, the Lamb of God, who takes away the sin of the world!" (Jn 1:29). He is the lamb who dies on a mountain just outside of the city of Jerusalem, providing salvation for the entire world.

Jesus' redemptive death changes everything. It fulfills the third covenant to bless all the nations. In doing so, our Lord makes each one of the four reactions in his day (and ours) obsolete. As Christians, no matter what we face in this post-Christian world, we are called to lovingly share God's good news with everyone.

Through his life and his ministry, Jesus seeks to restore the identity of Israel. Tomorrow we will look at Jesus' conversation with the Pharisees and how he shared his vision with them.

REFLECTION

1. Before you read this chapter, if someone had asked you to describe the identity and mission of the Church, what would you have said?
2. How does the story of the Jewish people change the way you look at the Church's identity and mission?
3. Why do we often have the same reaction to our enemies that the Jews had? Why is it easy to forget that our "enemies" are people we need to help save rather than people who are threatening our life or our freedoms?

DAY 18—FOUR

In week 1, we looked at the story of the prodigal son, and in particular, how the identities of the younger and older sons relate to the way we understand our identity today. Now I want to take a second look at this story because it is at the heart of Jesus' argument with the Pharisees about the Jews' identity and their call to be a blessing for the whole world to bring others to him.

As we saw in week 1, the story of the prodigal son comes in response to the Pharisees and scribes: "Now the tax collectors and sinners were all drawing near to hear him. And the Pharisees and the scribes murmured, saying, 'This man receives sinners and eats with them.' So he told them this parable" (Lk 15:1–3).

The Pharisees are questioning why Jesus eats with sinners and tax collectors. The Pharisees often had extra rules not found in the scripture, some of which were aimed at increasing people's devotion to the Law and many that clearly defined who was a Jew and who was not. The laws were meant to preserve identity at all costs, and Jesus' interactions with sinners and tax collectors present all sorts of red flags for the Pharisees.

In this parable, Jesus uses the character of the prodigal son to represent the sinners with whom he is eating. Not only this, but Jesus is telling the story of Israel. As we saw on day 17, the Jews went off in exile to a foreign country and were made slaves, just like the younger son. Jesus is announcing that the exile is now over and the captives can be welcomed home.

Jesus uses the indignant older brother in the parable as a different character. He has served his father faithfully at home while his brother squanders his inheritance and spends it on prostitutes. He protests the warm welcome his younger broth-er receives and refuses to join the party inside of the house. Jesus casts the Pharisees as this older brother (with Jesus him-self playing the merciful father). In doing so, Jesus reveals his worldview and his motivation for dining with the tax collectors and sinners. The Pharisees protest the return of the exiles to the Father's house, and because of their attitude, like the older son, they find themselves *outside* of the Father's house. The Pharisees have forgotten not only their own identity as sons but also the identity of the Father, who seeks out the lost and desires to bring his family members home again.

REVOLUTIONARY STORY

It's easy for us to accept the concept of the Father's merciful love for all, but it was a revolutionary idea to the Jews of Jesus' time because they had forgotten their identity. To the Jews, and in particular the Pharisees whom Jesus confronted, the Gen-tiles—the non-Jews of the world—were not people who needed to be saved. Rather, they were people from whom the Pharisees needed to be saved. This was the key misunderstanding of the Zealots and the Essenes as well. They thought they had to fight other nations or run away from them. Jesus' vision is that they love and convert other peoples.

When we recognize God's promise and Jesus' fulfillment of it, the gospels take on a whole new meaning. Black and white turn to color, and the stereo begins to blast out surround sound. Here are a few examples of how Jesus addresses the Jews' rela-tionship with the Gentiles:

- During the Sermon on the Mount, Jesus declares, "You are the light of the world. A city set on a hill cannot be hid. . . . Let your light so shine before men, that they may see your

good works and give glory to your Father who is in heaven"
(Mt 5:14, 16).

- In Luke 10, someone asks Jesus, "Who is my neighbor?"
(v. 29). He responds with the story of the good Samaritan,
which gives a surprising answer: A Samaritan, a non-Jew, can
be your neighbor. Later Jesus says, "You have heard that it
was said, 'You shall love your neighbor and hate your enemy.'
But I say to you, Love your enemies and pray for those who
persecute you" (Mt 5:43–44). Jesus wasn't telling people, "Be
nice!" He was reminding them that their enemies were the
people they were supposed to love.

- When Jesus enters the Temple courts (the place of power for
the Sadducees), he overturns the tables of the money changers. Why? Jesus tells us: "Is it not written, 'My house shall
be called a house of prayer for all the nations'? But you have
made it a den of robbers" (Mk 11:17). The money changers
were making it difficult for Jews and Gentiles from around
the world to worship at the Temple. They were more concerned with making money from them than helping them
worship God.

We see all of this culminate not only in Jesus' death, which
provides salvation to all people, but also in his last declaration
to his apostles before his Ascension: "Go . . . make disciples of
all nations" (Mt 28:19, emphasis added). Today, the Church still
has the mandate to work with Jesus to fulfill the third covenant.
The mission that God had for the Jews remains our identity and
mission today.

MODERN PHARISEES

Many scholars have noted that the story of the prodigal son ends
abruptly. The father confronts the older son, but we don't hear
the older son's final response. Will he come back into the house

and join the party, or will he stay outside the house protesting the younger son's return? I believe Jesus does this on purpose, leaving the Pharisees to come up with the ending. The choice is theirs. How will they conclude the story?

Just as it was a choice for the Pharisees in Jesus' day, it is a choice for us as well. In this post-Christian culture, it is very easy to act like the Pharisees, the Zealots, or the Essenes. Non-Catholics can become the enemy—someone to fight, escape, or argue with. We need to understand our differences, yes, but we must be careful not to repeat history.

As Jesus says in Matthew 23: "[The scribes and Pharisees] bind heavy burdens, hard to bear, and lay them on men's shoulders; but they themselves will not move them with their finger" (v. 4). And again later in this chapter, "But woe to you, scribes and Pharisees, hypocrites! because you shut the kingdom of heaven against men; for you neither enter yourselves, nor allow those who would enter to go in" (Mt 23:13).

It's not enough to only seek out our own holiness without ushering others into the kingdom. We can't create a bubble of holiness with extra rules and devotions that make it seemingly impossible for others to accept and live out the faith. We forget that we aren't just called to be holy; we are also called to be a light to the world.

In the words of Archbishop Charles J. Chaput: "When the world opposes Jesus Christ, we may end up being against the world. But in every such case, we're against the world for the sake of the world. After all, God so loved the world that he sent his only Son to save it, not condemn it. If we follow Jesus, we must love the world too and remain in it, as he did, to work for its salvation."[4] If we fail to reach out to others, we end up being condemned like the Pharisees, and like the older brother we find ourselves outside the Father's house.

Viewing God's identity and mission in the world incorrectly is one of the biggest threats to evangelization in our day. But we also have to be careful that as we relate to the culture, we don't make the mistake of the Sadducees—to give in to the culture so that we end up looking and acting like it. Tomorrow, we will discuss one area where many of us imitate the Sadducees today and how it threatens the work of evangelization.

REFLECTION

Take some time to sit and read the story of the prodigal son. While you may have read it many times before, this time read it in light of what you know about Jesus' mission to restore the identity of the Jewish people. Who do you identify with in the story? Have you ever felt like the Pharisees in being more concerned about your own personal holiness than the salvation of others? How do you hope to live out Jesus' story in your own life? The Pharisees are given a chance to respond differently. How will you respond?

DAY 19—FIRE

Imagine waking up suddenly in the middle of the night. As you snap to awareness, you realize that there is something seriously wrong in your house. You can't see anything, but you hear the blaring sound of the smoke alarm and you smell smoke in the air. As you pass through a chaotic darkness, you gather everyone in your house and get out the front door. While walking through your yard and onto the street, you notice that your house isn't the only one on fire on your block. Several other houses have started to burn. A few of your neighbors join you in the street, but there are several more people missing from the houses on fire. Perhaps they have already escaped and run to another part of the block. Perhaps they are still inside their houses and haven't made it out yet.

As you frantically contemplate what to do, you turn to one of your neighbors and ask, "Do you think there are people inside those houses? What should we do to try to get them out?" He responds, "I don't believe in fire. But even if fire exists, I think there are only a few people in life who are so weak that they can't make it out of their house." Confused and bewildered, you don't even reply but turn to another neighbor. Just then, the fire department shows up. You run up to them explaining the situation, implore them to check each house, and let them know that you are willing to do anything to help.

ETERNAL FIRE

Most of us would take every precaution to ensure that everyone made it to safety. At the least, we would probably approach each house and yell to the people inside. Some might even try to enter the houses to get people out. Yet when it comes to eternal fire, we aren't nearly as concerned about saving others. How much more important is eternal life than the one here on earth! I realize that this analogy, like all analogies, limps (even analogies about analogies limping do, in fact, limp). And yet I think there's a great deal of truth to it.

Many people in our world and even in our Church don't believe anyone goes to hell. If some people do, they are only the worst sorts of people—those on par with Hitler and Stalin. Our secular culture promotes tolerance as one of its highest virtues, and this tolerance often seeps into our religious beliefs. Like modern-day Sadducees, we find it easy to buy into the lies of our post-Christian culture and to not think of the eternal consequences of people's decisions.

But Romans 3:23 tells us "all have sinned and fall short of the glory of God," and Romans 6:23 states, "For the wages of sin is death." In a very real sense, everyone's house is on fire. We all face the prospect of hell without salvation from Jesus Christ and his Church.[5] While we don't know who is going to heaven and hell, and it isn't our job to judge people, we should adopt the attitude of people who see a house on fire: we should check to see if people are in harm's way and do whatever we can to help them. We should want to offer them the best route to safety—a relationship with Jesus Christ and his Church. To presume that everyone in a home is safe when there is a possibility that someone there will die is not charitable. It isn't nonjudgmental kindness. It's an extremely dangerous presumption!

JESUS ON HELL

What does Jesus himself have to say about hell? In the story of the prodigal son, when the father demonstrates just how far he'll go to show mercy to his wayward son, there's still a genuine realization of the need for salvation. The merciful father is very clear about the state of his sinful younger son when he replies to his older son: "For this your brother was *dead*, and is *alive*; he was lost, and is found" (Lk 15:32, emphasis added). The son wasn't physically dead, so the father must be referring to spiritual death. Next, the father and his younger son model the steps necessary to enter the father's house. The young son doesn't stay in the foreign country in sin. He doesn't just come home and receive the royal welcome. *He repents.* The father is merciful, but *he gives mercy to one who asks for it.*

How many people will go to hell? We don't know, but Jesus tells us this: "Enter by the narrow gate; for the gate is wide and the way is easy, that leads to destruction, and those who enter by it are many. For the gate is narrow and the way is hard, that leads to life, and those who find it are few" (Mt 7:13–14).

I could use many more passages of scripture to discuss hell and salvation. But it's crucial to include an insight from Ralph Martin on this topic: "The overwhelming theological interpretation of the texts of Scripture on the issue of salvation up until relatively recently has understood Scripture as saying that it is likely that the majority of the human race will be lost. This is the view of Irenaeus, Basil, Cyril of Jerusalem, John Chrysostom, Augustine, Aquinas, Canisius, and Bellarmine, as well as many others."[6]

The belief that hell may not exist or that very few people go there doesn't seem to come from Jesus or Church teaching but from our culture of tolerance. To buy into this idea is to imitate the Sadducees, men who were willing to accept the beliefs of their society in order to hold on to the power and admiration of the secular world.

Why does all of this matter so much? If we don't believe that hell exists, then we have little reason to evangelize. Why spend the time and energy to reach out to others? Why risk offending other people by inviting them to encounter Jesus? If there is no hell, our efforts are pointless. Our lack of conviction about hell is one of the key reasons we don't evangelize today.

HOW WILL WE SEE THE WORLD?

If we are honest, we will acknowledge that we have all been affected by the present culture in some way. It is the air we breathe and the water that we swim in. Its philosophy of tolerance and presumption of good in all things permeates our own worldview. In my own life, I can be tempted to give in to what the culture wants, as the Sadducees did. At other times, I can be like the Zealots or Pharisees. Each of these reactions affects my attitude toward evangelization and the way I live out the identity that God wants for me.

How, then, shall we live? We can start by following amazing examples of evangelization and by praying that the Lord will renew our hearts. We will cover these topics in our next two chapters.

REFLECTION

1. In the story of the fire, we all want to be the person who seeks to save others. Why do you think our attitudes change when the topic turns to eternal salvation?
2. What do you believe about hell? What role do you think the culture has in shaping this view?
3. How do your beliefs about hell change the way you think about your relationships with other people?

DAY 20—EXAMPLE

Anjeze Gonxhe Bojaxhiu was born the youngest of three children on August 27, 1910, in Skopje, Macedonia (formerly Yugoslavia). When Gonxhe was young, she was fascinated by stories of missionaries. In fact, she could locate different missions on a map and tell others what was going on in each location. During her teenage years, she was so moved by stories of the work done by the Yugoslav Jesuit missionaries serving in Bengal, India, that she decided to become a religious sister in a missionary order.

Gonxhe joined the Sisters of Loreto and moved to Ireland for formation. She would never see her family again. Inspired by St. Thérèse of Lisieux (the patroness of missions), Gonxhe took the name Sr. Mary Teresa. The world would know her by this name, although with a slight variation. After she gained experience and became a superior, she became known as Mother Teresa, and eventually, St. Teresa of Calcutta.

MOTHER TERESA, THE TEACHER

Following her formation, Mother Teresa moved to the Indian city of Calcutta and became a teacher at the Loreto convent school there. For twenty years, she taught at this school, eventually becoming the headmistress. One of her companions at the time noted that Mother Teresa "was a very hard worker. Very. Up to time on this, up to time on that. She never wanted to shirk anything, she was already ready."[7] Mother Teresa not

only served her students during this time but the poor as well,
especially on Sundays.

> "Every Sunday I visit the poor in Calcutta's slums. I cannot
> help them, because I do not have anything, but I go to give
> them joy. . . . In that 'para'—that is how a group of houses
> is called here—twelve families were living. Every family has
> only one room, two meters long and a meter and a half wide.
> The door is so narrow that I hardly could enter, and the ceil-
> ing is so low that I could not stand upright. . . . Now I do not
> wonder that my poor little ones love their school so much,
> and that so many of them suffer from tuberculosis." Then,
> she would pray, "O God, how easily I make them happy!
> Give me strength to be always the light of their lives and so
> lead them to You!"[8]

A SECOND CALLING

Had Mother Teresa continued this work of teaching and visiting
the poor, her life would have been extraordinary enough. And
yet her story would take a dramatic turn in September of 1946
during a train ride for her annual retreat. What happened on
this train was the foundation for what would become Mother
Teresa's life work and the motivation for everything that she did.

While on the train, Mother Teresa received what she calls
"a second calling," or "a call within a call." It was a call to leave
her life as a teacher and to serve the poorest of the poor in the
slums of Calcutta. Not only would she serve the destitute but
she would also call other sisters to do the same. Mother Teresa
formed a new order, the Missionaries of Charity, whose goal
was "to satiate the thirst of Jesus Christ on the Cross for Love
and Souls" by "laboring at the salvation and sanctification of the
poorest of the poor."[9]

I THIRST

The focus on Jesus' thirst is rooted in Mother Teresa's meditation on Jesus' words "I thirst," spoken on the Cross at Calvary. While Jesus had a physical thirst, Mother Teresa perceived that Jesus' thirst was spiritual as well. He thirsted for love and longed for souls to come to know him.

In her own words: "Why does Jesus say 'I thirst'? What does it mean? Something so hard to explain in words— . . . 'I thirst' is something much deeper than just Jesus saying 'I love you.' Until you know deep inside that Jesus thirsts for you—you can't begin to know who He wants to be for you. Or who He wants you to be for Him."[10]

After consulting with her spiritual director, she sent a letter to her archbishop: "During the year very often I have been longing to be all for Jesus and to make other souls—especially Indian, come and love Him fervently—to identify myself with Indian girls completely, and so love Him as He has never been loved before."[11]

MOTHER TERESA'S CRITICS

Mother Teresa is one of the greatest icons of the twentieth century. She received the Nobel Peace Prize in 1979 and became a household inspiration the world over. But she is not without her critics. Steven Pinker, a professor of psychology at Harvard, asks in a *New York Times Magazine* article, "Why do so many people admire Mother Teresa?"

Pinker explains that Bill and Melinda Gates have used their resources to provide far more aid and eliminated far more diseases than Mother Teresa. He wonders, "Why don't they receive more admiration than this so-called saint?"

In response to Pinker, Gary Anderson points out, in his book *Charity*, that people do not value Mother Teresa for her productivity or efficiency but for her faith.[12] While Bill and Melinda Gates may bring better health to more people than Mother Teresa and her sisters, *they don't risk anything*—their lives aren't really affected. The same couldn't be said of Mother Teresa—she risked everything and gave her whole life for the poor. Her work came from a deeply held faith in the way God sees the world and how he wants it to be. She believed that God (whom she couldn't see) thirsted for these souls, and she gave everything to answer his call. This is true faith, one that makes almost anyone envious, no matter your religious or nonreligious background.

When it comes to living out the mission that Jesus calls us to, we face difficult questions. Like Mother Teresa, are we willing to live out Jesus' vision for the salvation of the world, even when we can't see it? Are we willing to not just say that we love others and wish they would come to know him but to do something about it? Are we willing to go beyond our comfort zones to live a faith that costs us a great deal? The amazing thing is that Jesus faced these same questions. In the next chapter, we will see how he responded to this immense challenge and what it means for how we respond as well.

St. Teresa of Calcutta, pray for us!

REFLECTION

Consider Mother Teresa's words about Jesus' desire for us: "Until you know deep inside that Jesus thirsts for you—you can't begin to know who He wants to be for you. Or who He wants you to be for Him."

Week 1 of this book considered the theme of encounter. While this week is focused on a vision for evangelization, our encounters with our Lord are primary and are in fact the impetus of our evangelization to others. Take some time to contemplate Jesus' thirst for you on the Cross and the love with which he died for you. Truly, there's no point in seeking out the lost in love if we aren't in intimate contact with the one who loves us.

DAY 21—GARDEN

Throughout his life, Jesus knew that his mission was to die for the salvation of the world. All that he was experiencing as a result of his decision to go through with this sacrifice comes to a crescendo during his agony at the Mount of Olives.

> And he came out, and went, as was his custom, to the Mount of Olives; and the disciples followed him. And when he came to the place he said to them, "Pray that you may not enter into temptation." And he withdrew from them about a stone's throw, and knelt down and prayed, "Father, if thou art willing, remove this cup from me; nevertheless not my will, but thine, be done." And there appeared to him an angel from heaven, strengthening him. And being in an agony he prayed more earnestly; and his sweat became like great drops of blood falling down upon the ground. And when he rose from prayer, he came to the disciples and found them sleeping for sorrow, and he said to them, "Why do you sleep? Rise and pray that you may not enter into temptation." (Lk 22:39–46)

The Agony in the Garden occurs directly after the Last Supper. At the Last Supper, Jesus not only establishes the Eucharist during the Passover but also tells his disciples that one of them will betray him. Knowing that the hour of his betrayal and death is fast approaching, he heads to the Mount of Olives, where he is staying while he visits Jerusalem (Lk 21:37).

Once on the Mount of Olives, Jesus prays to his Father to remove the cup from him. The cup symbolizes the trial that Jesus is about to undergo for the salvation of the world—his betrayal, suffering, and death.

At the heart of this passage is the intensity of prayer that Jesus experiences. Luke describes Jesus as being in agony to the extent that "his sweat became like great drops of blood" (Lk 22:44). While this description sounds very odd to us at first, the mixture of blood with sweat is a physiological phenomenon that has been scientifically verified in people under immense stress.

JESUS' MEDITATION

I think the key question for this passage and for our meditation is, What does Jesus think about during this time of prayer that causes such stress?

First, it's clear that Jesus has intimate knowledge of the sufferings that he will undergo. As a Jew living in the Roman Empire, he is well aware of the excruciating pain he is about to suffer. Jesus is divine, but he's also human, and any human would shudder at the idea of being tortured and crucified.

Second, our Lord is aware of the intense spiritual battle that awaits him. Scripture tells us that the devil is closely involved in this whole process. The trial that Jesus faces is to endure not only physical pain but spiritual pain as well. It's also important to keep in mind that Jesus is tempted to escape all of this suffering. He is God. At any point, he could escape this trial through his own power.

WEEPING OVER JERUSALEM

Jesus' actions and words just days before this moment give us insight into what is going through his mind. Luke describes Jesus weeping over the city of Jerusalem as he recalls how his people have rejected him and the punishment that will come upon them for their hard hearts (Lk 19:41–44). I believe these thoughts weigh heavily on Jesus as he prays in the garden before his crucifixion.

OUR AGONY IN THE GARDEN

Knowing Jesus' thoughts during this time are crucial, but the actions of the disciples, especially Peter, can really help us apply this scene to our own lives. During this week, we've looked at four types of reactions to the Roman occupation—those of the Essenes, the Zealots, the Sadducees, and the Pharisees. Peter exhibits the behavior of each of these groups during the Agony in the Garden and subsequent events. As Jesus is captured, Peter plays the role of the Zealot, pulling out a sword and cutting off the ear of the high priest's slave (Jn 18:10). He plays the role of the Essene as he escapes from the scene and into the night (Mt 26:56). He is like the Sadducees when he is accused of being one of Jesus' disciples and gives up his integrity out of fear (Mt 26:69–75). And he is like the Pharisees when he locks himself in the upper room with the other disciples as they strive for survival in a hostile world (Jn 20:19).

While each of these actions helps us understand the temptations that Peter experienced in the surrounding culture, most striking to me are his actions during Jesus' prayer. During Jesus' intense agony over his imminent Passion and Death, Peter and the other disciples fail to pray with him. They are asleep, seemingly indifferent to the Lord's mission and the sacrifice before him. It is so easy for us to do the same. We can deny it, escape it, or explain it away, but the challenge remains: Will we join our Lord in his mission or will we seek our own?

The rest of this book is an attempt and a journey to reach the world today as Jesus did in his own age. I invite you to step into the garden with Jesus, to see the world from his perspective, and to live out the true identity of the people of God.

REFLECTION

For today's reflection, pray the first Sorrowful Mystery of the Rosary, the Agony in the Garden. As you pray, imagine the scene with Jesus and his disciples. Where are you in the scene? Are you willing to pray with Jesus? Do you want to fall asleep with the disciples? Do you want to walk away? Feel free to meditate on this scene longer, praying more decades of the Rosary or in silence. Ask the Lord for the desire and conviction to stay with him and to join his mission.

WEEK 4—EQUIPPED

DAY 22—SPIRIT

So far we've been through twenty-one days together. Great job getting this far; you're more than halfway through!

During the first week, we looked at Jesus' encounters with his first disciples and how to have an encounter with him today. In week 2, we examined what it means to be a disciple of Jesus—what habits and characteristics we need to be a follower of him. Week 3 hopefully challenged you to see the world as Jesus does. We explored the different reactions to the secular culture in Jesus' day and how they relate to our post-Christian world today. And on day 21, we joined Jesus in the Garden of Gethsemane. Like his disciples, we had a choice to join him in his mission or to walk away.

My hope and prayer is that you decided to wholeheartedly join Jesus in his mission. When God calls us to something more, it is very normal for us to not know the next steps. Often we are paralyzed by questions and fears. As I mentioned in the introduction, when I was called to work for FOCUS, I had this same experience. Even now, God continues to call me into a deeper relationship with him as I reach out to others. While my experience and knowledge have increased over the years, I still don't always know how I'm going to pull everything off.

The same was true for Jesus' first disciples. After Jesus' death on the Cross—the sacrifice that God had promised to Abraham that would allow the Jewish people to become a blessing to all the nations—he rises from the dead and charges his followers to "make disciples of all nations" (Mt 28:19). It's time for them to not only know their identity but also to live it out. There's just one problem—after Jesus calls his disciples to take up this great mission, he leaves them. How can they live out what Jesus has called them to do?

THE HOLY SPIRIT FOR ALL NATIONS

Scripture doesn't make us wait long for an answer. In the Acts of the Apostles, chapter 2, on the Jewish feast of Pentecost, all the apostles are together in one place when "suddenly a sound came from heaven like the rush of a mighty wind, and it filled all the house where they were sitting. And there appeared to them tongues as of fire, distributed and resting on each one of them. And they were all filled with the Holy Spirit and began to speak in other tongues, as the Spirit gave them utterance" (vv. 2–4).

The Holy Spirit fills the apostles and then it does something really interesting—it enables them to speak other languages. This may seem odd until we remember Jesus' vision for God's people and the need to make disciples of all nations. How can the apostles make disciples of all nations if people can't understand what they are saying? Fortunately, the feast of Pentecost gives them a great chance to test out this new gift. Jews from around the world had gathered in Jerusalem for the feast, and upon hearing the apostles, they understand them in their own languages (Acts 2:8). When Peter preaches the Gospel, three thousand of these Jews are baptized in one day (Acts 2:37–41).

BETTER THAN JESUS

The story of Pentecost reveals that God wants to give us the Holy Spirit so that we can reach the world with the Gospel. In fact, having the Holy Spirit within us is even better than having Jesus by our side. Don't believe me? Jesus said it himself! "Nevertheless I tell you the truth: it is to your advantage that I go away, for if I do not go away, the Counselor will not come to you; but if I go, I will send him to you" (Jn 16:7). Jesus is very clear: It's a good thing that I'm leaving you because then the Holy Spirit (the Counselor) will come to you.

RECEIVING THE HOLY SPIRIT

The most pronounced way that Catholics receive the Holy Spirit is through the Sacrament of Confirmation. The *Catechism* outlines the effects of this great sacrament:

- It roots us more deeply in the divine filiation, which makes us cry, "Abba! Father!"
- It unites us more firmly to Christ.
- It increases the gifts of the Holy Spirit in us.
- It renders our bond with the Church more perfect.
- It gives us a special strength of the Holy Spirit to spread and defend the faith by word and action as true witnesses of Christ, to confess the name of Christ boldly, and never to be ashamed of the Cross. (*CCC* 1303)

While the Holy Spirit comes to us in a special way through Confirmation, we need to continually receive the Holy Spirit. How do we do this? In the Gospel of Luke, Jesus provides a valuable lesson on the importance of *asking*, and it applies directly to the Holy Spirit.

> And I tell you, Ask, and it will be given you; seek, and you will find; knock, and it will be opened to you. For every one who asks receives, and he who seeks finds, and to him who knocks it will be opened. What father among you, if his son asks for a fish, will instead of a fish give him a serpent; or if he asks for an egg, will give him a scorpion? If you then, who are evil, know how to give good gifts to your children, how

much more will the heavenly Father give *the Holy Spirit* to
those who ask him! (Lk 11:9–13, emphasis added)

One of the best ways to receive the Holy Spirit is simply to
ask for him. And Jesus tells us to think of the Holy Spirit as a
gift. God wants to give us his good gifts, but like most fathers,
he is much more inclined to give them when his children ask
(or even beg).

Pope Benedict XVI, in a homily during World Youth Day
2008, gave us insights on the Holy Spirit as a gift that we can ask
for on a daily basis: "Yet this power, the grace of the Spirit, is
not something we can merit or achieve, but only receive as pure
gift. God's love can only unleash its power when it is allowed
to change us from within. We have to let it break through the
hard crust of our indifference, our spiritual weariness, our blind
conformity to the spirit of this age. Only then can we let it ignite
our imagination and shape our deepest desires."[1]

As you contemplate your desire for the Holy Spirit and perhaps feel that "hard crust" of indifference, spiritual weariness,
and blind conformity to this post-Christian world, I pray that
God gives you the Holy Spirit in abundance, a gift that the Father
so deeply desires to bestow on you. Find time for prayer each
day and be sure to ask for the Holy Spirit to come into your life,
particularly as you strive to be a disciple of Jesus.

REFLECTION

At Pentecost, our Lord gave the Holy Spirit to the apostles to
enable them to make disciples of all nations. The Holy Spirit
equipped them to evangelize to *the challenge in front of them*.
What challenge is in front of you right now? What prevents you
from living out Jesus' mission in your own life? Read Acts 2:1–13
and ask God for an outpouring of the Holy Spirit in your life.

DAY 23—FORTITUDE

As we begin the journey of evangelizing others, one thing almost always stands in our way—fear. Sharing the faith can be difficult. We may worry about what others will say and think about us, or perhaps we're concerned that our efforts will get in the way of other things that we enjoy.

One of the most beautiful aspects of our faith is that God gives us just what we need to respond to his call. Last chapter, we saw how he gave the apostles the ability to speak in tongues in order to preach the Gospel to the nations. But this isn't the only gift he gave us at Pentecost. The Church tells us that there are seven gifts of the Holy Spirit: wisdom, understanding, counsel, fortitude, knowledge, piety, and fear of the Lord.

To confront our fear, especially of obstacles that stand in our way, fortitude is the gift of the Holy Spirit that we need the most. Listen to this definition of fortitude: "*Fortitude* is the moral virtue that ensures firmness in difficulties and constancy in the pursuit of the good. It strengthens the resolve to resist temptations and to overcome obstacles in the moral life. The virtue of fortitude enables one to conquer fear, even fear of death, and to face trials and persecutions" (*CCC* 1808). If the prospect of evangelizing conjures up fear, then it's fortitude that you need!

ON FEAR AND FORTITUDE

We see the gift of fortitude on display after Jesus' Death. Before Pentecost, the apostles lock themselves away, scared to be in public. Afterward, they boldly proclaim the name of Jesus to the masses. In particular, the author of Acts, Luke, recounts the actions of Peter and John after Pentecost. Through the power of the Holy Spirit, they begin to heal the sick and preach the Gospel around the Temple.

In Acts 4, the Sadducees, who control the Temple, arrest Peter and John for teaching the people about Jesus' Resurrection from the dead (remember, they were sad, you see, because they didn't believe in an afterlife). After the Jewish officials question them, they "*called* [Peter and John] and charged them not to speak or teach at all in the name of Jesus" (Acts 4:18, emphasis added).

I find it interesting that the Jewish officials *call* Peter and John not to speak in Jesus' name. While Jesus calls us to share our faith and make disciples of all nations, their culture then, and our post-Christian culture now, call us to stop proclaiming the name of Jesus.

We need fortitude to resist the pressure of the world and fulfill his mission, and this is exactly what Peter and John have. Even under threat of imprisonment and death, they can't help but share Jesus with others: "We cannot but speak of what we have seen and heard" (Acts 4:20).

This need for fortitude rings true in my own life. Most people don't know this, but I'm an introvert. Telling others about the faith and standing up for what I believe do not come naturally to me. Most nights I'd love to be at home with a good book all by myself. But I know that I'm called to do something more. I'm called to overcome the obstacles in my own temperament as well as those I find while reaching out to others. I've encountered Jesus in such a powerful way that I know I can't let my temperament or personal preferences stand in my way. I need fortitude again and again if I'm going to persevere in sharing my faith.

PRACTICAL STEPS

So, what are some ways that we can live out this gift of fortitude in our everyday lives? Here are three practical ways to begin the evangelization process:

1. *Bring up the faith naturally in conversation.* The faith doesn't have to be something that we just share from the *Catechism* or the Bible. In conversations with friends, we can talk about our encounters with God. Sometimes hearing someone profess what God is doing in their life, especially in difficult and frustrating times, serves as a powerful witness. Our faith isn't just about being happy all the time; it helps us through difficult moments as well. This witness allows others to see how the Gospel can play a role in their lives when they are struggling the most.

2. *Charitably witness to the faith on issues that are hard to discuss.* This can be difficult to do. We can have two polar-opposite reactions when a sensitive issue comes up. On one hand, we may be tempted to say nothing. We convince ourselves that we don't know enough about the topic or will hurt someone else's feelings. On the other hand, we may decide to state the truth but without considering how our words make someone else feel. Fortitude enables us to overcome both of these reactions and share the truth in love. Sharing the truth in love is a gift that is acquired over time. Using fortitude to dive into these conversations helps develop the muscle we need to have hard but meaningful discussions with others.

3. *Invite others to participate in the faith.* Almost every act of evangelization starts with an invitation. When we hear that something isn't going well in someone's life, we can offer to pray for them. Even if they aren't practicing Christians, we can invite them to pray with us as we pray for them. Very few people turn down the offer for prayers! We can extend invitations to non-Christians to hang out with our fellow

Christians so that they can experience another way of living. We can invite others to Bible study or Mass. These small invitations, which require fortitude, develop in us an openness to hearing and accepting bigger invitations down the road.

Each one of these moments may evoke some fear in us. But we must realize that in each one, God is with us. Whenever the people of God are sent out on a mission, they are told to not be afraid. From Moses to David to Mary, God tells them, "Do not be afraid," and reminds them that he himself is with them. Remember, this is what the Holy Spirit is all about—the promise that God will be with us, even to the end of the age. The gift of fortitude is a reminder that when we are afraid, God is right by our side, ready to help.

REFLECTION

When you picture yourself sharing the faith with others, what are you most afraid of? Consider the worst possible scenario and call on the Holy Spirit to give you fortitude. Pray, "Jesus, I trust in you."

DAY 24—FRIENDSHIP

Yesterday we considered one of three important actions we can perform as disciples—practicing fortitude. Today, we'll look at another important action for evangelization: friendship. In the Acts of the Apostles, I don't think it was a coincidence that Peter and John evangelized together. I'm sure they formed a close friendship while traveling with Jesus for three years.

Not only that, but Jesus showed them how important friendships were as he shared the Gospel. Jesus was friends with sinners, tax collectors, Jewish leaders, fishermen, and all sorts of people in the communities he visited. He ate with them, traveled with them, and talked to them. Friendship was a powerful staple of his ministry.

So what does this friendship look like? How can we characterize friendships within the Christian faith and those that help us evangelize others? Rather than drawing on an example from the ancient world, today I want to look at a twentieth-century saint who was amazing at friendship: Pier Giorgio Frassati.

Pier Giorgio Michelangelo Frassati was born into an influential and well-off family in Turin, Italy, on April 6, 1901. From a very young age and throughout his university years, Frassati showed a deep faith in Jesus and the Church. He was known for his devotion to the Blessed Eucharist, his all-night vigils in adoration, and his daily prayer life.

When we think of Italian Catholicism in the past, we may imagine that this type of faith was very normal for his time, but in reality, Frassati lived in a post-Christian culture. During his life, the Church was under attack, first by the Communists and then by the Fascists, who eventually rose to power during World War II under Mussolini. Many Catholics were persuaded by these ideologies, which were often anti-Church and anti-clerical. Frassati's own father was an agnostic, and his mother was a nominal Catholic who advised him against receiving daily Communion out of fear he would become a priest.

In this hostile climate, friendship was Frassati's main weapon to build up his fellow Catholics and to evangelize others. He was someone whom everyone wanted to be around. In his university's Christian society (Cesare Balbo Circle) he was known as "[the] member who, without looking for the honour, possesses innumerable friends and enjoys a pleasant authority over them, who knows each and is beloved by each, puts himself out to please them, accepts every duty and carries it out to the general satisfaction."[2]

He cultivated these friendships by inviting others into the things he loved. He was a man who enjoyed mountain climbing, skiing, smoking his pipe, and playing practical jokes on his friends. Through his loyalty, his infectious laugh, and his willingness to embark on any adventure, he built deep, rich, and impacting relationships.

Within these relationships, he invited others to experience his greatest possession—his faith. He encouraged his friends, acquaintances, and even strangers to go to Mass and to love our Lord despite the hostile culture around him. He had no fear, and his charity and friendship enabled him to invite people into a deeper relationship with Jesus. One of his friends, struck by his ability to attract others, remarked, "His secret for gaining hearts and souls was his unalloyed charity."[3]

PERIPHERIES

Frassati's charity extended beyond those in his circle, seeking those on the peripheries, especially the poor. As we saw on day

13, having friendships with the poor is one of the most effective ways to share the Gospel.

Here's one account of how Frassati lived this out.

> One night, at one o'clock in the morning, [he] came into the printing works, streaming wet from the rain. He had come from Borgo San Donato on foot, because he had not a penny for the tram. He had not a penny because he had spent the night with a sick old woman and emptied his pockets on her table. He went often to Cottolengo, the big hospital in Turin. . . . Pier Giorgio went into the wards and talked to the patients—his brothers, as he called them—consoled them, brought them money, things to eat and clothes, and never hesitated, being a total stranger to all human repulsion and fear of contagion, to put his arms around them.[4]

As a child of the Italian upper class, Frassati often received spending money from his parents, but he chose to give much of it away to his impoverished friends. He would routinely give up meals, train tickets, his vacations, and even his coat in the dead of winter for the sake of the poor. Upon his high school graduation, his father offered him the choice of a car or the equivalent in money. He chose the money so that he could give it away.

As his days as a student were coming to a close, and he was very near to the completion of his engineering degree, Frassati contracted the deadly poliomyelitis virus (polio), most likely during his work with the sick. Though he was dying at the young age of twenty-four, Frassati went joyfully to his eternal reward in heaven. Even in his final days, he showed his care and regard for others as he scrawled out, in weak and shaky handwriting, instructions for getting vaccinations for a poor sick man he had been caring for. To the end, Frassati was friendship personified—in the face of death, in his care for the poor, and in his love for the Lord. He teaches us the value of friendship in the ordinary situations of life.

COURAGEOUS FRIENDSHIPS

In the Gospel of John, Jesus says, "Greater love has no man than this, that a man lay down his life for his friends" (15:13). Bl. Pier Giorgio was a good friend to so many people. He was a man who, through his character and his interests, was someone whom everyone wanted to be around. We need to strive to be a friend such as this. Are we the kind of person that others want to be around? Do we love others with a selfless love?

Then, are we willing to be courageous in these relationships like Bl. Pier Giorgio? Are we willing to share with our friends the greatest gift that we have—our faith? And are we willing to make friends with those on the periphery—the poor, the lonely, the outcast? Friendship is one of the most powerful weapons in evangelization. We must be willing to lay down our lives for our friends.

Tomorrow we will look at a third important action for disciples, invitation to community. We will see how the dynamic of friendship plays out on the community level as an important tool in evangelization.

Bl. Pier Giorgio Frassati, pray for us!

REFLECTION

1. What about the example of Bl. Pier Giorgio stood out to you? Is there anything that you wish to incorporate more into your own life?
2. What kind of friend are you? Do you have a selfless love that impacts those around you?

DAY 25—COMMUNITY

At Pentecost, the first Christian community was formed by the three thousand people who were baptized that day. Fellowship was one of the four key characteristics of this early Church: "And they devoted themselves to the apostles' teaching and fellowship, to the breaking of bread and the prayers" (Acts 2:42). In this book, we covered the apostles' teachings (the kingdom) on day 10, fellowship (friendship) yesterday, the breaking of the bread (sacraments) on day 11, and prayer on day 12. As we saw yesterday, friendship is not only something to build up fellow Christians but also a means of evangelization. In the Acts of the Apostles, these key characteristics also led to spreading the Gospel: "And day by day, attending the temple together and breaking bread in their homes, they partook of food with glad and generous hearts, praising God and having favor with all the people. And the Lord added to their number day by day those who were being saved" (2:46–47).

This community lived out their faith and invited others into it. How do we do this in our post-Christian culture today?

ALPHA

If you go to London and stand at the intersection of Cromwell and Brompton on a Wednesday night, chances are you'll see a stream of people walking to a church in the quaint neighborhood of South Kensington around 7 p.m. They will shuffle past the gloriously built Catholic Oratory to a smaller, humbler building behind it, an Anglican church called Holy Trinity Brompton.

Almost every Wednesday night of the year, up to six hundred people arrive here, most of them in their twenties and thirties—many who have never stepped inside of a church before. They come for the Alpha Course that runs three times each year and offers a basic introduction to Christianity and a dynamic presentation of the Gospel.

I'm not sure about your church, but I know mine can't draw six hundred nonbelievers on a weeknight, maybe not within an entire year. And, chances are, the culture in London is more hostile to the faith than yours. A recent poll of those in London recorded that 43 percent of the population was Christian, 49 percent had no religion, and 8 percent were of non-Christian religions, mostly Muslim.[5] A few years ago, the Anglican Church, England's most prominent religious presence, was coming to grips with the alarming exodus from its ranks. The question for its leaders was not "Can we keep our church from a drastic decline?" but rather, "What is the best way to manage this drastic decline?" In other words, how do we close down our churches, schools, and other establishments in the best possible way?

And yet in the midst of this crisis and in the midst of an increasingly agnostic and disbelieving culture, the Holy Trinity Brompton community continues to fill its church with nonbelievers of the most difficult demographic (young people) who are eager to hear the Gospel. How do they do it?

HOW DID ALPHA BEGIN?

The story of Alpha begins with a man named Nicky Gumbel. Gumbel is the humble and gregarious pastor of Holy Trinity Brompton. Raised in an agnostic Jewish home, Gumbel considered Christianity irrelevant, false, and boring. While a university student, he met a group of Christians, and to disprove their faith, he started to read the New Testament. After reading all of it, he determined that it was true, and soon after, he gave his life to Jesus Christ. Through his experience at Holy Trinity Brompton, he was moved to become a full-time minister and was ordained a priest in the Anglican Church. He continued to serve Holy Trinity Brompton and in 1990 began running the Alpha Course, previously a class for new parishioners. Gumbel modified the course to make it attractive to nonbelievers as well as churchgoers.

WHAT HAPPENS AT ALPHA?

In Gumbel's own words, "[The Alpha Course] is an opportunity to explore the meaning of life in a very low-key, nonthreatening, unpressurized environment. People come for a meal, they hear a talk, they have coffee, and then they discuss with a group of people who like themselves are totally outside of the church."[6]

What does Alpha cover? Gumbel notes that they start with the big questions: "Who am I? Where did I come from? Where am I heading? Does this life have a meaning? Does it have a purpose?"[7] Starting where their audience is, the Alpha Course answers these questions—not with vague references to Christianity but with a bold presentation of the Gospel and how it can bring meaning to people's lives. The ultimate goal is to wrestle with Christianity's answers to these questions and then to cultivate an openness to an experience of the Holy Spirit. Over nearly three decades, through a number of different churches across the globe, 29 million people have tried Alpha in 169 countries and 112 different languages.[8] Today many Catholic parishes sponsor "Alpha for Catholics" courses that present the Gospel through the Catholic lens.

WHAT'S THEIR SECRET?

The growth is not by accident. Everything in Alpha is intentional and strategic. From the meal, to the presentations, to the conversations, to the training of leaders, Alpha seeks to build a culture of reaching out to others. In reality, this is the "secret" to Alpha. While it features a world-class presentation of the Gospel, a structured program, and a dynamic marketing plan, Alpha ultimately succeeds or fails based on those who run the course.

The community that runs Alpha can't just be any community; they must live out many of the things that we have discussed so far in this book. They are people who have truly encountered Jesus, often through the Alpha Course itself. They are people who know the power of relationship and seek to invite their friends and to befriend those that come to the course.

When Christians establish a community like this, it creates a culture of evangelization that is sorely missing from many of our parishes. Often, when Catholics think to evangelize, their first step is to invite former Catholics or non-Catholics to Mass. But former Catholics often left because they didn't value Mass, and it is very difficult for non-Catholics, especially non-Christians, to appreciate our liturgy. The Mass was never intended to evangelize. In fact, in the early Church, nonbelievers weren't allowed to stay for the sacred mystery of the consecration—a tradition still practiced today when people go through RCIA and, to a greater degree, in some Eastern Catholic liturgies.

A community like this creates a space for people within and outside of the Church to ask questions about their faith that they may otherwise be afraid to ask. It allows them the opportunity to put their doubts, fears, and difficulties on the table to wrestle with them and to invite God and others into the conversation. It creates a space for people within a parish to invite friends, family, and acquaintances to experience the faith in a healthy and nonpressured way.

For those who attend Alpha or help lead it, the community becomes a model for what faith should look like: a faith that is willing to ask questions *and* seek answers. A faith that invites Jesus to be an active participant in all aspects of life. A faith that doesn't stop at our own experience, but that seeks out the lost to share the Good News.

Communities are vital for evangelization. They can range from a formal setting such as a Newman Center or a parish to a group associated with a particular program or retreat, such as Alpha. Faith communities can be as simple as a group of friends who love Jesus and invite others into this friendship to experience and question the Christian faith lived out. No matter what the format may be, we aren't meant to evangelize on our own. Communities help us live out the faith and share Jesus with others.

REFLECTION

1. How does your parish approach those outside of the Church? How do you think it could improve these efforts?
2. What can you personally do to create or encourage a culture of community-based evangelization in your parish or among your Catholic friends?

DAY 26—STORY

This week is all about equipping you to evangelize. Day 22 looked at the Holy Spirit as the principal agent of evangelization. Over the last three days, we have discussed three steps we can take to evangelize others—be courageous, develop friendships, and invite others into a community. These offer us the chance to share our faith, but when we have these opportunities, what do we say? As we follow along with the apostles in the Acts of the Apostles, they each have a story to tell. A story about how Jesus' Death and Resurrection changed everything, and a story about how their own lives changed as a result. Over the next three days, we will learn how to share God's story and our story just like these first apostles.

THE STORY BEHIND THE NAME

Before we do that, it's essential to understand just how important stories are, especially for our post-Christian culture today. I discovered this firsthand while naming my children. In Catholicism, we traditionally name our children after saints, whether it be their first or middle name. This saint gives them a story to live out and a model for the Christian life. When my son was born, we needed to select a name for him. The year was 2008, and Pope Benedict had declared it the year of St. Paul. As a missionary family, we figured that Paul would be a great name and that St. Paul provided an exemplary story and model for our son's life.

As a parent, I have found that one of the most exciting aspects of naming your children is explaining your choice when they ask you. For my son Paul, this happened when he was three and his sister, Mary Clare, was five. They had been looking at an old-school children's Bible, one with pretty intense pictures (at least for small children). On one page, St. Paul was preaching to the crowds. On the next, a man stood with a sword drawn over St. Paul with his neck exposed. Mary Clare wanted to know what was going on in the pictures. Before I could explain, she asked, "This is who you named Paul after, right?" I told her yes and then went on to explain that St. Paul was a missionary, which meant he told people about Jesus. Some of the people he spoke to didn't like that, and so they beheaded him . . . which meant they cut off his head. Then, an unforgettable conversation ensued.

> Mary Clare: Dad, aren't we missionaries?
> Me: That's right.
> Mary Clare: Don't we tell people about Jesus?
> Me: Um . . . yes, that's right.
> Mary Clare: Dad . . . are they going to come and kill us too?

WHAT AM I TO DO?

Stories have the power to change our lives in ways that we don't anticipate. By naming my son Paul and connecting his life to this great saint, a powerful narrative was established that my children quickly absorbed.

The philosopher Alasdair MacIntyre, in his work *After Virtue*, notes: "Man is in his actions and practice . . . essentially a storytelling animal." He goes on, "I can only answer the question, 'What am I to do?' if I can answer the prior question 'Of what story or stories do I find myself a part?'"[9] Philosophers normally try to help us answer questions about our existence: Who are we? Why are we here? How should we live? MacIntyre says that man ultimately answers these questions through story. Humans are wired for story. We live out the stories we hear and the stories that people communicate with their lives.

By the way, just one day after the episode with the story of St. Paul, I came up to my son's bedroom to tuck him in for the night. I found him kneeling down by his bed with a play sword at his neck. I asked, "Paul, what are you doing?" He quickly responded, "I'm getting beheaded!" Stories are powerful. They play a huge part in how we live!

STORIES AND EVANGELIZATION

Now that we know the amazing power that stories have to shape lives, we turn to the topic of evangelization. Practically, how can we use this great tool?

One of the most important claims that we can make to our post-Christian world is that there is a story. Archbishop Charles J. Chaput states, "The 'truth' of our time in the world seems to be that there is no truth, that life has no point, and that asking the big questions is for suckers. . . . Thus the Church's task is to tell and retell the world its story, whether it claims to be interested or not."[10] In sum, people are made for living out stories, and in a world that tells them that they have none, we have a prime opportunity to tell them the greatest story ever told, one that gives them meaning and purpose.

How do we tell this story? Before we speak any words, the primary way that we tell a story is with our lives. We demonstrate our meaning and purpose with the choices we make each day. People see this. They watch how we live. They see how we deal with stress, handle our money, study for classes, discipline our children, and interact with everyone from our spouse to the mail carrier.

Next, we have to fill our lives with great stories if we are going to live great stories. I've tried to employ this method throughout this book. We saw how stories influenced the lives of the saints—remember Augustine being affected by the story of St. Anthony of the Desert. I hope you've seen your own life affected by the stories of St. Teresa of Calcutta and Bl. Pier Giorgio Frassati. When we hear great stories, stories that inspire us, we want to emulate them. We want to live them out.

We also need to be careful about the stories that we consume. It's so easy to end up living the story of our world, which tells us to be comfortable, make lots of money, and live out "our passion" (whatever that might be). Some people wonder why it is difficult to live the Christian life, but at the same time they fill much of their time watching stories that tell an entirely different worldview. These stories don't have to be rated R to have a negative impact on us. They just have to tell a different story than that of the Gospel.

In the end, the question is, What story are you living? If people looked at your life, would they see the story of someone trying to live like Jesus? Would they know that you are someone who desires to know Jesus and make him known?

Finally, we want to use stories to share the Gospel. Jesus knew the power of stories and wasn't afraid to share revolutionary messages through stories in his day. Typically Jesus did this through parables. As we saw with the story of the prodigal son, he tells parables to share God's worldview and to show how different it is from that of the people he speaks to.

How do we share the Gospel through stories today? Over the next two days I'll show you specific ways to share God's story and your story with others.

REFLECTION

1. What stories do you consume on a regular basis? How do they influence you?
2. Have you ever thought of your life as a story? What kind of story are you living?

DAY 27—GOD'S

Throughout this week, we've been looking at how the early apostles lived out their calling to make disciples of all nations. In the first few chapters of Acts, we see the disciples share the story of Jesus over and over. (Some examples include Acts 2:14–36; 3:11–26; 7:1–53; 8:5, 35.)

In the tradition of the Church, we have a name for this story: the kerygma. The kerygma is the core message of the Gospel, an initial proclamation of what we believe. John Paul II reminds us: "The vital core of the new evangelization must be a clear and unequivocal proclamation of the person of Jesus Christ, that is, the preaching of his name, his teaching, his life, his promises and the Kingdom, which he has gained for us by his Paschal Mystery" (*Ecclesia in America*, 66).

While we see the example of the apostles and hear the importance of sharing this story from our Church, many Catholics don't know how to tell this story in a clear and confident way. There are several ways to share the kerygma, but I want to show you a way to present God's story through five simple steps.

These five steps are rooted in the teachings of the Church and the teaching of St. Catherine of Siena, a Doctor of the Church. St. Catherine had mystical conversations with Jesus, and in one of these conversations, Jesus gave her a clear way of understanding our salvation. This explanation has come to be known as the Bridge Illustration.

These five steps can be shared on a napkin in a bar during a sixty-second conversation or over the course of a Bible study. (FOCUS does this in a Bible study that I wrote called "The Crux:

Exploring a Relationship with Jesus Christ and His Church." You can download it for free at focusequip.org.) Below I'll include some pictures from the Crux to help you tell God's story to others.[11] While these illustrations appear simple and straightforward, many people have told me that seeing the Gospel drawn out and explained in this way has produced a light bulb moment when they finally understood the faith and how to incorporate it into their lives.

STEP 1—WE WERE CREATED FOR RELATIONSHIP

FOCUS leaders begin the kerygma by sharing the narrative of Genesis to show that "in the beginning" God created us for a relationship with him. God, our Father, created us out of love and for love. During the Crux, FOCUS leaders draw a circle to show completeness and to symbolize the way our relationship was with God in the beginning.

STEP 2—THIS RELATIONSHIP IS BROKEN

When people hear that we are made for a relationship with God, they may have two conflicting feelings. The first is that there is truth to what is said. As we saw above, there's a God-shaped hole in each one of us that longs for something more, and suggesting that this longing is for God can resound with others.

At the same time, some people feel very distant from God. They may not positively identify God as their heavenly Father because of their own broken relationship with their earthly father. They may have some loss or suffering in their lives that is connected to that relationship.

In the Crux, FOCUS leaders draw a jagged line through the circle. What was once complete now feels broken. Almost everyone can relate to this brokenness in their life. The question: What's the answer to this brokenness?

STEP 3—JESUS IS THE ANSWER

Steps one and two are extremely important. We want to speak to people where they are and to the emptiness they often feel. Only by recognizing the problem does a solution make sense. After establishing that we are made for a relationship and that this relationship is broken by sin, FOCUS leaders explain that Jesus is ultimately the answer. He is the one that provides a solution to the problem of sin that we all experience.

Many people are confused about why Jesus had to die and how this affects us. This is where we can use our diagram again.

When we left off, our circle was cut in half by a jagged line because of the brokenness that comes with sin. We now draw a new image (see below). We explain that because of sin there is a gap between man (on the left) and God (on the right). No matter what we do (indicated by the arrows), no matter how good we are, we can't cross this divide on our own. It is an infinite chasm because there's a problem: God and sin cannot mix. There has to be a solution other than ourselves.

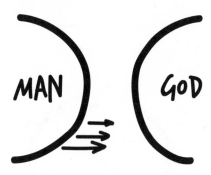

This answer is Jesus' Death on the Cross. Because Jesus is fully human, he can represent the human family and offer an act of love on our behalf. However, because he is fully divine, his act of love on the Cross takes on infinite value. Thus, Jesus can bridge this infinite divide. His death gives us an opportunity to overcome sin, to live as God's sons and daughters, and to go to heaven. To bridge the chasm, FOCUS leaders now draw the Cross in the middle.

STEP 4—WE ARE INVITED INTO RELATIONSHIP WITH GOD

Jesus is the answer that allows us to restore our relationship with God, but he can't make this decision for us. God invites us into this relationship. He is a perfect gentleman. He offers, but he doesn't force us. The choice is ours, and we need to make a definitive decision for him. We can illustrate this invitation by drawing a line across the divide to show how we can get across.

Here it's helpful to ask people questions about where Jesus is in their lives. Is he in their life at all? Is he one of many things in their life? Or, is he Lord of their life? Is he their number 1 priority? In addition to this question, it is helpful to ask not only where they are but also where they want to be.[12] This question helps you see their heart, and it can often reveal the obstacles they have in accepting the Gospel into their lives.

STEP 5—WE ARE CALLED TO LIFE IN THE CHURCH

Finally, we aren't just called to have a personal relationship with Jesus. Ultimately, our relationship with our King is found in a relationship with his kingdom, the Church. We are not called into one-on-one relationships with Jesus; we are called to live in the family of God. We live out this family life through many of the things we have studied in this book—the sacraments, fellowship with other believers, the teachings of the Church, and prayer, to name a few. As people come to accept Jesus, we can help them understand their next steps. If they are already Catholic, typically Confession is the next best step for them. If they aren't Catholic, RCIA is a good option for them to consider. To illustrate all of this, FOCUS leaders draw a circle with the Church inside. On earth, restoration with God occurs through the Church.

REFLECTION

God's story is worth sharing well. And if we are going to evangelize others, we need to know what to tell them. For your reflection today, take some time to study how God's story was told above and how you might explain it to someone else. Don't be afraid to practice—on friends who are faithful and eventually on friends who aren't.

When we tell God's story, many times people ask for our own. What will we tell them? We will tackle that tomorrow.

DAY 28—YOURS

Pope Paul VI once said, "Modern man listens more willingly to witnesses than to teachers, and if he does listen to teachers, it is because they are witnesses" (*Evangelii Nuntiandi*, 41). When someone claims to be Catholic or to teach a part of the faith, modern man often leans in and asks, "Okay, but what do *you* really believe?" and "Do you *really* live this out, or is it just something you talk about?" Our culture today is very sensitive to hypocrisy. People want to know what you actually believe and how you actually live, not just some theory or vague ideal.

This is what makes testimonies so valuable. Through them, we tell our stories in a way that shows Catholicism has affected our lives. Far from making our lives look perfect, our testimonies allow us to show where we've been, what God has done, and how we are still trying to work out all the details. Our stories make the faith tangible, authentic, and seemingly possible. When we tell our stories, people think about their own stories and what their lives might be like with God more involved. They see that we found faith or transformation and wonder if this might be possible for them. We can't underestimate the power of our stories.

So how do we tell them?

Ultimately, storytelling is an art form, and there's no perfect method, but through my work with FOCUS, I can offer some specific recommendations and questions to think about as you prepare your testimony. Continuing this week's theme from the Acts of the Apostles, we'll use Paul's testimony in Acts 26:1–29. Here are four steps for telling your story. Feel free to go back and read Paul's testimony for greater insight.

STEP 1: YOUR LIFE BEFORE JESUS (ACTS 26:1–11)

Who were you before you met Jesus? What did you think about
the faith? How did you perceive Christianity? Were you raised
in the faith or outside of it? What was that like?

STEP 2: HOW YOU CAME TO KNOW JESUS (ACTS 26:12–18)

What happened that caused you to see a change in your life?
What did you understand differently? How did you feel at that
moment? Perhaps your pivotal moment involved a retreat, a
marriage, the birth of a child, the loss of a job, a friendship that
went wrong. You may have had a gradual conversion over time,
but you should still be able to pick out one or two key moments
for your testimony. These key moments will help your audience
grasp what you decided to do and why. No need to overdrama-
tize your story. Sometimes simple stories are encouraging to
others who think someone has to be hit over the head with a
lightning bolt to have a conversion.

One tip for this part of the story: Really think through the
details and what is necessary and what isn't. Keep the details that
build suspense or tension and leave out the ones that distract,
confuse, or aren't appealing to your audience.

STEP 3: YOUR LIFE IN JESUS CHRIST (ACTS 26:19–23)

What is your life like now that you have made a deeper commitment to Jesus? Concretely, how do you live differently? There's no
need to come across as a person with a perfect life or someone
whose life is still in shambles. It can be helpful to share a little of
the good and bad in an authentic way.

An additional tip for this part of your story and throughout
your testimony: avoid Catholic jargon. Many times when we

have a deeper relationship with Jesus and come to know more about the Church, we begin to use Church language that many people don't understand. If you talk about how you gave full assent to the reality of transubstantiation during the benediction of eucharistic adoration, people will be distracted and confused. Use language that everyone can understand and relate to.

STEP 4: CHALLENGE AND INVITE

In some way, you want to ask those listening, "What do you think?" or "What's your reaction to Jesus?" In casual conversations, I like to ask, "What's your experience with spirituality or Christianity?"

BUT I'M NOT GOOD ENOUGH

As you read through the four steps and consider your own story, you may begin to make excuses. You may think something such as, "My story isn't good enough," "I'm not good at sharing my story," "My story is too boring," "My past is too crazy," or "I'm not holy enough."

St. Paul, one of the greatest evangelists, has this to say: "When I came to you, brethren, I did not come proclaiming to you *the testimony of God* in lofty words or wisdom. For I decided to know nothing among you except Jesus Christ and him crucified. And I was with you in weakness and in much fear and trembling; and my speech and my message were not in plausible words of wisdom, but in demonstration of the Spirit and of power, that your faith might not rest in the wisdom of men but in the power of God" (1 Cor 2:1–5, emphasis added).

The fact of the matter is this: Like St. Paul, we don't need to have it all together. We don't need the perfect story. But we do need to tell others what God has done in our lives. We do need to be willing to witness to the Cross and its power to save everyone in this world. Our own story together with God's story make a powerful one-two punch in witnessing to Jesus Christ.

REFLECTION AND TESTIMONY

As you consider these four steps, pray about your own life and your conversion. Take out a sheet of paper and write down your thoughts on each step.

After your time in prayer, go ahead and work toward having a story that you can tell others when you feel called to share your faith. Ideally, your story will be around three to five minutes long. Sometimes you'll only have sixty seconds to share it with someone, other times much longer. Even if we don't share our story right away, it's good for us to reflect on God's actions in our life and the moments of encounter and conversion that we've experienced. Being grateful for these moments makes it easier and more natural to share what he's done for us.

WEEK 5–
DISCIPLE-MAKERS

DAY 29—WIN-BUILD-SEND

Congratulations! You've made it to the last week. If you remember, way back in the introduction to this book I laid out a road map for our journey through the lens of WIN-BUILD-SEND. Let's review where we've been so you know where we will go during this last week.

The first week was all about WIN. We looked at the theme of *encounter*. Before we can follow Jesus or ask others to follow him, we must first encounter our Lord. This was his method of reaching others. He didn't simply share wisdom or philosophical platitudes but gave people encounters with the living God. The men and women he helped lived from these encounters and often followed Jesus as a result. The same should be for us. Like the early disciples, we need to reencounter the Lord as we continue this process.

The second week was all about BUILD. We focused on what it means to *follow* Jesus. As disciples, we learned to follow the rabbi and imitate him. We can't just call ourselves disciples; we must think and live differently. We need to cultivate basic habits of disciples such as daily prayer, participation in the sacraments, and care of the poor.

The third and fourth weeks were all about SEND. In week 3, we discussed a vision for evangelization. God promised to reach the entire world through Abraham and his offspring, and Jesus fulfilled this promise through his ministry, Death, and Resurrection. We have the opportunity to join Jesus in this mission as we seek to share the Good News.

In week 4 we learned to equip ourselves to evangelize through the power of the Holy Spirit. We looked at three ways we can begin the evangelization process and three actions we can perform as disciples in telling others about Jesus. Knowing some simple things to do and say can go a long way in evangelization.

While the WIN-BUILD-SEND model is an amazing vision for how to live out and share the faith, there's another aspect of evangelization that makes it all come together in a dynamic way, and that's exactly what I want to share with you this week. It's the most important and crucial part of this entire process. Let's go back to the story that we've seen unfold in the early Church. This time, let's take a look at the ministry of St. Paul.

ST. PAUL'S METHOD

St. Paul was the greatest evangelist the Church has ever seen. Soon after his conversion, he began telling others about Jesus and risking his life for the sake of the Gospel. While many of the apostles were focused on sharing the faith with the Jewish people, Paul was given a particular mission to speak to the Gentiles to help fulfill the promise that God made through Abraham to bless all nations. In the Acts of the Apostles, Paul notes that God told him, "I have set you to be a light for the Gentiles, that you may bring salvation to the uttermost parts of the earth" (13:47).

When we think of St. Paul, we normally imagine him as evangelizing the world by himself. We picture him in synagogues and temples preaching on his own. We think of the letters he wrote by himself to the many churches that he visited. But in reality, there was much more to Paul's method of evangelization.

What we often don't realize is that Paul typically had other disciples at his side that he was training. Remember Jesus' method of discipleship that was practiced by the Pharisees? Before his conversion, Paul was a Pharisee who studied under one of the greatest rabbis of his day, Gamaliel (Acts 22:3, Acts 5:34).

It's hard to think of a better person to lead the charge in making disciples of all nations! From his training, Paul knew how to teach the faith, and how to raise up disciples who would imitate him and share the faith on their own.

Once we grasp Paul's method, we begin to see it play out in his life. For instance, if we read the Acts of the Apostles closely, we detect the names of many men that he mentored throughout the Roman Empire. These include Silas, Barnabas, John called Mark, Gaius and Aristarchus of Macedonia, Timothy, Erastus, Sopater of Beroea, Aristarchus and Secundus of Thessalonica, Tychicus and Trophimus of Asia, and Luke (the author of the Acts of the Apostles).

WHAT DID HE TELL THEM?

Paul not only trained his disciples as he traveled the known world but also planted them in various places to build up the Church. Paul tells us in 2 Timothy 4 that he sent Tychicus to Ephesus and Erastus to Corinth, and left Trophimus at Miletus. Paul would visit these disciples on his subsequent journeys, or when that wasn't possible (like when he was in jail), he would write to them. Through Paul's letters to Timothy and Titus, we get an inside look at how Paul evangelized and what he told others to do as well.

In 2 Timothy, Paul reminds Timothy: "Follow the pattern of the sound words which you have heard from me, in the faith and love which are in Christ Jesus" (1:13). Like other rabbis and disciples, Paul wants Timothy to imitate him. As Paul notes in 1 Corinthians, "Be imitators of me, as I am of Christ" (11:1).

But then Paul goes one step further—*and this is the key to this entire week*—he tells Timothy, "You then, my son, be strong in the grace that is in Christ Jesus, and what you have heard from me before many witnesses entrust to faithful men who will be able to teach others also" (2 Tm 2:1–2). To Titus he says something very similar: "This is why I left you in Crete, that you might amend what was defective, and appoint elders in every town as I directed you" (Ti 1:5).

St. Paul instructs Timothy and Titus on how to extend their discipleship. The method of rabbis and disciples wasn't simply to live out the faith, or to live out the faith and share it with others. The model was to live the faith, share the faith, and raise up other disciples who could do the same. This is exactly what Timothy and Titus are told to do. As disciples of Jesus who are called to make disciples of all nations, we are supposed to do this as well.

I realize that the idea of making disciples can be overwhelming and intimidating. Many people think, "I can't do that!" But this book focuses on *everyday disciples* because I want to show you that this is something that almost anyone can do in their current state in life and situation. This last and vital step is what this week is all about. First, we'll see why making disciples is so important. We'll look at three reasons for disciple-making and three objections to it over the next two chapters. After that, we'll consider two stories that show how this model is possible in everyday life. Finally, I'll help you brainstorm practical ways to carry it out and give you some inspiration for moving forward.

REFLECTION

1. Were you surprised at how many different people St. Paul trained as his disciples? Why do you think he was so passionate about bringing people along with him?
2. What does evangelization look like to you? How does your view compare to Paul's?

DAY 30—WHY?

Throughout this book, we've seen the example of disciple-making from Jesus and St. Paul. When they were faced with the question, "How can I best reach the entire world with the news of the Gospel?" making disciples was a key part of the answer. If we share their desire to evangelize, then how can we not seek to follow their example?

And yet, this last step can be difficult. In a post-Christian world, simply living out our faith is hard enough. Sharing our faith takes even more courage. And being an example for others of how to live and share the faith seems almost impossible at times. Is it really necessary?

When we decide to do difficult things, we may be tempted to give up in the face of obstacles. In those moments of doubt or frustration, we need motivation to keep going. We need to know why what we are doing is essential. In this chapter, we look at three reasons why making disciples is so important.

REASON #1—DISCIPLE-MAKING ENSURES PEOPLE KEEP THE FAITH

While we've been talking about discipleship in the context of evangelization, disciple-makers are important for the entire WIN-BUILD-SEND process from start to finish. This type of mentoring is essential as people come to faith and learn to live it out, especially in our post-Christian world.

If you've been involved with ministry for any period of time, you've probably witnessed what happens without disciple-making. Maybe you've seen large numbers of people come to faith through conferences, retreats, Catholic education, sacramental prep, or youth ministry. Even though these events serve a great purpose, when we look back five years later, many times we wonder, "Where did all those people go?" As in the parable of the sower (day 14), people hear the Word, "but the cares of the world, and the delight in riches, and the desire for other things, enter in and choke the word, and it proves unfruitful" (Mk 4:19). One of the best ways to ensure that the Word isn't choked is to place someone of faith in this person's life. Someone who can walk with them through good times and bad. Someone who can answer questions and give them practical answers. Someone who can call them to something greater when they are beginning to give in to the world. Someone like a disciple-maker.

While we might see great numbers and moving responses with large group events conducted by a charismatic leader, we have to seriously consider the long-term effects of using this method by itself. The power of mentorship is crucial for keeping the faith, and disciple-makers have the training to effectively help others over time.

REASON #2—EVANGELIZATION IS TAUGHT AND MODELED

At the end of the parable of the sower, Jesus notes what happens to those who are planted in good soil: "[They] hear the word and accept it and bear fruit, thirtyfold and sixtyfold and a hundred-fold" (Mk 4:20). As you've seen in this book, we are all called to evangelize. As Pope John Paul II made clear, "No believer in Christ, no institution of the Church can avoid this supreme duty: to proclaim Christ to all peoples" (*Redemptoris Missio*, 3).

Many Catholics don't evangelize because they don't know how or are too afraid. Sharing the faith must be learned by watching someone else do it. By seeing someone model evangelization, we realize that it is possible in a very practical way. Disciple-makers model evangelization for others so that they can share the faith with others (and also show others how it's done). This seems like the only reasonable way that we can bear fruit thirty-, sixty-, or a hundredfold.

REASON #3—DISCIPLE-MAKERS CAN FULFILL GOD'S PROMISES

As we seek to fulfill God's desire to preach the Gospel to everyone on earth, we should recall that there are *almost eight billion* people alive today, and this number continues to grow. How can we reach them all?

One of the coolest things about disciple-making is that it allows the faith to grow exponentially. This exponential aspect creates a reasonable way to reach everyone on earth, as God desires. Let's look at the math.

Let's say that someone made three disciples in a year, and then the next year those three disciples made three disciples each. After two years, there would be twelve new disciples, which isn't all that impressive compared to eight billion people.

But let's fast-forward to see how this method works over time. Keep in mind that each disciple makes only three other disciples. In other words, an individual doesn't keep making disciples year after year; they just make disciples once.

After five years, there would be 243 disciples. After ten years, more than 59,000. Then, after fifteen years, 14 million. After twenty years, more than 3 billion. And, after thirty years, more than 10 billion people. [1]

This kind of exponential growth is powerful. I realize that humans aren't perfect and that conversion and discipleship don't always happen quickly. But if we are going to reach the entire world with the Gospel, exponential growth is essential. (Note that exponential growth doesn't have to happen just with individuals. It can also happen through communities and groups who work together to see people come to faith and raise them up to reach others.)

Imagine if someone made more than a million disciples in one year. That would be an amazing movement of the Holy Spirit! But, even after thirty years, the result would be only 100 million Christians. The world adds 130 million souls to our planet *each year*. Even if someone made 100 million disciples *each year* they wouldn't be able to keep up.

While God can reach the world however he likes (he once converted 9 million Mexicans through Our Lady of Guadalupe), one practical way that we can reach everyone in the world is if all Catholics respond to their call to evangelize and to take up the task of making disciples. Remember, this isn't just some human method made up in the twenty-first century to efficiently reach the world; it was Jesus' own method from the beginning! God had a master plan for evangelizing the world that he modeled for us on earth. We are called to follow his example. Making disciples is not easy. There will be trials. There will be setbacks. There will be failure. But it's worth it!

REFLECTION

1. If someone asked you why they should practice disciple-making, what would you say?
2. If you still have difficulties with this concept, what is holding you back? Write it down and have an honest conversation with God about it.

DAY 31—OBJECTIONS

Yesterday I gave you three reasons for disciple-making. Over the years, I've heard many objections to living out this model. In this chapter, I want to address some of the questions that people ask in response to the concepts in this book. No matter what your opinion is, I'm passionate about having a dialogue on how we can best reach the entire world with the Gospel in a post-Christian culture. My hope with this chapter is to contribute to that dialogue and to wrestle with how to do it within the reality of the Church and world today. I'm sure I don't have all the answers, but I do know that I want to work with others to find them.

OBJECTION #1—WE HAVEN'T EVANGELIZED LIKE THIS IN THE PAST; WHY NOW?

While the biblical narrative paints a picture of disciple-making that was common to the early Christians, over time Catholics developed some specific structures for evangelization that looked quite different.

To start, evangelization and sharing the faith were largely delegated to the clergy. Because of the need to limit heresy and teach the faith correctly, the Church put the communication of the faith in the hands of those who were formally educated and trained to do so. The laity was called to evangelize, but typically within the family. Parents were expected to pass on the faith primarily to their children. We created institutions such as the parish and Catholic schools that were responsible for passing on the faith in a corporate rather than personal, way.

These methods of sharing the faith were not the result of Catholic teaching but rather became custom over time. They also made sense within the context of a primarily Christian culture. While we need well-trained clergy who evangelize, parents who bring up Christian children, and vibrant parishes and schools to pass on the faith, our post-Christian world calls us to do even more.

In many ways, Vatican II sought to change the customs that had developed, including those of evangelization. To respond to the need for evangelization in a post-Christian world, the Church called for the laity to return to the method of the early Church. Vatican II's *Decree on the Apostolate of the Laity* (*Apostolicam Actuositatem*) states, "The apostolate of the laity derives from their Christian vocation and the Church can never be without it. Sacred Scripture clearly shows how spontaneous and fruitful such activity was at the very beginning of the Church. . . . Our own times require of the laity no less zeal: in fact, modern conditions demand that their apostolate be broadened and intensified" (1).

Later on, this same document states, "[The laity] bring to the Church people who perhaps are far removed from it, earnestly cooperate in presenting the word of God especially by means of catechetical instruction, and offer their special skills to make the care of souls and the administration of the temporalities of the Church more efficient and effective" (10). This vision aligns with the vision presented throughout this book, especially in regard to disciple-making.

Modern sociology backs up the conclusions of Vatican II concerning the role of the laity. In their thoroughly researched book *Young Catholic America: Emerging Adults In, Out of, and Gone from the Church*, Christian Smith and his coauthors emphasize that a relationship with someone else who practices the faith (such as a relative or youth minister) is the most important factor in helping a young person keep the faith. In reference to institutions such as the parish and schools, Smith notes: "Sociologically speaking, religious institutions, programs, and practices matter because they foster and guide these relationships. In the absence of such relationships, the institutions, programs, and practices can feel empty to teens and thus *become almost totally ineffective*" (emphasis mine).[2]

Disciple-makers are needed. Our post-Christian world shows us that different models are needed than the ones we have used in the last few centuries, and the tradition of evangelization in the early Church is something we can rely upon as a sure guide to moving forward.

OBJECTION #2—CAN'T WE JUST USE THE INTERNET?

Over the last three decades, the advent of the internet has brought all sorts of positive advances to our lives. In the past ten years, the use of smartphones has taken technology to a whole new level as we seem to have an app for everything and are in constant communication. When it comes to evangelization, there is often a temptation to export this task to online programs, videos, or other tools.

While it can be effective, this method also has its limitations. Maybe an analogy will help. Throughout the centuries, armies on the ground were typically used to fight and win wars. Over the last hundred years, planes and other flying devices have proved to be a tremendously powerful tool to fight wars. At the same time, very few major battles are won by the air force alone. In the end, an army has to go into battle, take over key buildings, and force the enemy to surrender. The same is true with evangelization. While the internet can be an extremely useful tool, ultimately soldiers on the ground are needed to bring about conversions. Videos, programs, and websites help, but most people need another human being to show them how to live their faith. When we encounter issues or challenges in our faith, it is important for us to have an actual person to care for us and show us the way. The internet can't substitute for real human contact.

OBJECTION #3—EVANGELIZATION JUST ISN'T MY THING

Usually, the reasoning behind this objection is that someone doesn't feel as if they can evangelize others and make disciples. They think it just isn't who they are or how God has wired them. In reality, many could say the same about parenting.

If you talk to most new parents, the idea of bringing children into this world and raising them in the faith seems daunting. But parents learn that over time they are given the grace for the task. Something they feel entirely ill equipped to do becomes possible.

Evangelization works the same way. God gives the grace to accomplish this seemingly impossible task. You never feel perfectly comfortable or entirely equipped, but as with parenting, your conviction that this is what you are supposed to do drives you to figure out the task and to ask God for help. We know from scripture and Church teaching that we must evangelize. We just need the courage to actually go and do it.

Over the next three chapters, I want to continue to help you learn how. Tomorrow we look at how a simple Polish tailor used the power of disciple-making to change the world.

REFLECTION

1. What objections do you have to making disciples? Were they answered in this chapter? If not, how can you continue this discussion?
2. What would disciple-making look like in your own life?

DAY 32—JAN

St. John Paul II was one of the most influential figures of the twentieth century and one of the greatest popes the Church has ever known. He traveled the globe more than any other pope in history, some 775,000 miles, or more than three times to the moon. More people saw him than any other person in human history as he visited 129 nations on 104 journeys. His writings, which equal the length of twenty Bibles, include fourteen encyclicals, fifteen apostolic exhortations, eleven apostolic constitutions, forty-five apostolic letters, twenty-eight motu proprios, and several bestselling books. He was a poet, a playwright, and even had a CD go platinum, selling more than one million copies.

While his accomplishments are profound, his character and his ability to relate to others stood out to many. The famous theologian Yves Congar, who wrote the following at Vatican II about then-archbishop Karol Wojtyla, well before his papacy, perhaps said it best: "[He] made a remarkable impression. His personality dominates. Some kind of animation is present in this person, a magnetic power, prophetic strength, full of peace, and impossible to resist."[3]

St. John Paul II was an amazing human being, but before his time in office, people invested in him deeply to help him become the man who would change the world and so many lives.

A TIME TO STEP UP

During his teenage years, Karol Wojtyla lived in Krakow, Poland, and grew up in St. Stanislaw Kostka parish, a dynamic church run by the Salesian Fathers. During the German occupation of Poland, the Nazis rounded up eleven of the thirteen priests from the parish and sent them to concentration camps. Without much choice, the two remaining Salesians leaned on their parish community to pick up the slack, and an unassuming and surprising man stepped forward.

Jan Tyranowski was not a likely person to lead the youth of the parish. He was a quiet tailor and a loner, a lifelong celibate who lived with his mother. He spoke formally, often sounding like a walking catechism text, and had eccentric mannerisms and a high-pitched laugh. Despite all of this, Jan became the most effective lay leader in his parish.

THE SECRET OF JAN TYRANOWSKI

What was Tyranowski's secret?

First, Tyranowski had an amazing prayer life characterized by deep encounters with the Lord each day. In 1935, he was already a devout Catholic when he heard a sermon where the priest told the congregation, "It's not difficult to be a saint." From this point forward, Tyranowski dove into daily meditation and developed a powerful spirituality. St. John Paul II later described him as "one of those unknown saints, hidden amid the others like a marvelous light at the bottom of life, at a depth where night usually reigns. He disclosed to me the riches of his inner life, of his mystical life. In his words, in his spirituality, and in the example of a life given to God alone, he represented a new world that I did not yet know."[4]

The second part of his secret was his method of reaching the young men of St. Stanislaw Kostka: Living Rosary groups.

George Weigel, in *A Witness to Hope*, a biography of St. John Paul II, explains, "The Living Rosary as created by Jan Tyranowski consisted of groups of fifteen young men, each of which was led by a more mature youngster who received personal spiritual direction and instruction from the mystically gifted tailor."[5]

Each week, Tyranowski held an hour-long meeting in his apartment to teach his group the fundamentals of the spiritual life and ways to improve their daily lives. Eventually he would mentor the four group leaders or animators, Karol Wojtyla included. These group leaders then led their own groups of fifteen (one member for each mystery of the Rosary, as there were only fifteen mysteries at the time). In addition to this, all sixty men met with Tyranowski on a monthly basis to hear him speak.

FROM KAROL WOJTYLA TO POPE JOHN PAUL II

Before meeting Tyranowski, Karol Wojtyla did not think of joining the priesthood. Under Tyranowski, it became an irresistible option, despite protests from many people around him. Wojtyla's good friend, Malinski, said this about Tyranowski: "I can safely say that if it weren't for him, neither Wojtyla nor I would have become priests."[6] In fact, over the years, ten men who were in Tyranowski's Living Rosary groups joined the priesthood.

As a priest, Wojtyla no longer faced the Nazis but rather the Communists who oppressed the Polish people. He continued to live out Tyranowski's method, forming Living Rosary groups and mentoring the leaders. He accompanied university students through Mass, lectures, and camping. Eventually these deep friendships created a tight bond, and the group began referring to themselves as *Rodzinka*, meaning "little family." Wojtyla hiked, skied, camped, and kayaked with them, all the while challenging them spiritually and intellectually. He stayed in contact with many of these men and women during his papacy, sometimes inviting them to the Vatican or his summer retreat house, as he continued to accompany them throughout their lives.

As we look at the work of Tyranowski and Wojtyla, we realize that at a time when their Catholic and Polish identities were threatened by post-Christian worldviews, they refused to hide who they were. Rather, they knew it was a moment of great need for evangelization. They knew that our Lord was calling them to share their incredible devotion with others. Whether they were working with a member of the clergy or a layman, using small-group and personal discipleship was key to inflaming hearts.

Like Jesus and St. Paul, they knew that personally mentoring others was the most effective way to produce disciples who love God and want others to know him as well. This is what a disciple does. The example of a disciple is invaluable, enabling people to model their lives off one another and not only to be faithful but fruitful as well.

REFLECTION

1. Jan Tyranowski didn't have extraordinary gifts or talents to reach people, and yet he was incredibly effective. What was his secret?
2. Tyranowski and Wojtyla both believed it was important to spread the faith during Nazi and Communist occupation. Why were they both willing to do this despite the risks?

DAY 33—KEVIN

Before we close this book, I think it's important to share with you more of my own story. I was born and raised Catholic in a midwestern home. My parents did a fantastic job of sending me to Catholic schools, going to Mass on Sunday as a family, and being involved in our parish. They showed me the importance of our faith throughout my childhood, but my faith didn't become meaningful to me until after grade school.

Like many kids, I didn't fully understand the faith and got into my fair share of trouble. While I knew right from wrong, I didn't really grasp why it all mattered. But, also like many teenagers, I was looking for purpose and meaning in my life. My brother and sister were both involved in a Protestant youth group, and over time I began going to different meetings. The summer before my freshman year of high school, I heard a speaker named Scott Anderson give a very clear presentation of the Gospel (like the one we talked about on day 27) and his testimony (like we saw on day 28).

For the first time, my eyes were open—Jesus died on the Cross *for me*. I finally understood God's love for me, and I faced a definitive question: If Jesus gave himself up for me on the Cross, what was I doing in response?

I answered this question by changing my life drastically. Around this time I was confirmed, and I chose the name Paul because I likened my conversion to his. While my testimony isn't dramatic from the outside (like Paul's), this encounter with Jesus was the pivotal moment that changed everything. I began praying each day. I found ways to let go of many sins and attachments in my life. I changed most of the friends that I hung out with and began going to youth group each week.

As I progressed through my high school years, I was certain that God wanted me to share his story just as Scott had shared his story with me. I didn't know what God wanted me to do, but I knew I needed to tell others about him no matter what career I chose. During my first two years of college, I went to a public university on the East Coast majoring in religious studies and philosophy. The Catholic fellowship was lacking, but I made friends with many wonderful evangelical Protestants on campus. I eventually transferred to Benedictine College in Atchison, Kansas, where I studied theology and philosophy and began dating the woman I would marry. Wanting to learn how to play a bigger role in the New Evangelization that Pope John Paul II called for, I spent the next two years in graduate school at the Augustine Institute.

EVANGELIZATION AND DISCIPLESHIP IN THE REAL WORLD

As I mentioned in the introduction, it was after graduate school that I joined FOCUS. After spending two years doing missionary work on campus, I went to FOCUS's headquarters to work in the curriculum department in 2009 to write Bible studies and other resources for the organization. But even when I fundraised my salary and had a full-time job working for a Catholic missionary organization, I was not excused from living out evangelization and discipleship outside of work.

Over the years, I've tried several different methods within our parish. I've led Bible studies in my home and in prisons. I've had strategic conversations with directors of religious education, pastors, and parish staff about what evangelization can look like in the parish. I've learned a lot about what can work and what doesn't work. Recently I feel like I've seen WIN-BUILD-SEND play out in my parish, and below I'll share five key elements that help my parish community live out evangelization.

MY OWN PARISH STORY

First, we are part of a parish that embraces the idea of evangelization, small groups, and discipleship. It is so important for us to be supported by our pastor—in his encouragement, his homilies, his staff, and the programs that he seeks to run. This is probably our biggest blessing.

Second, we set up a place of encounter in our parish where we can WIN people to the faith. For us, this is the Alpha Course. It gives a space in our parish where we can invite all people to consider a relationship with Jesus and his Church. Some of our members attend Mass weekly, but others have come to our parish to understand more about the faith or have been invited by a coworker, friend, neighbor, or family member who is in the parish.

Third, we begin the BUILD stage by looking for the fruit that comes from Alpha. If people make a commitment to Jesus or show an interest in going deeper, there are several options for them. They can go to RCIA if they aren't Catholic or if they need to understand the faith on an intellectual level. If they enjoy Alpha, they can attend again or help out an Alpha table leader. Also, they can join a small group and learn how to live out their faith from other believers.

Fourth, we look to SEND the people that we've built up who are ready to evangelize and make disciples of others. This involves personally investing in them through discipleship. Normally, we start out by building up a friendship with these people. We may invite them to our home or out for a meal. Over time, we ask them if they'd be willing to commit to a more formal discipleship time where we hold them accountable and train them in evangelization.

Finally, we look to have these people go on to do mission themselves. The Alpha Course is key to this step as well. It is a concrete area where we can ask people to lead. All the while, we are right there with them to give them additional training and help along the way. We continue to work with them until they are making disciples themselves and understand what to do.

This is just one way to live out the WIN-BUILD-SEND model. Tomorrow we will consider how this mindset changes the way we view what may currently exist in our parishes and how to create a practical plan to live this model.

REFLECTION

At this point, I realize that you might be overwhelmed. Take some time to give your worries to our Lord. Realize that God wants to reach the whole world so much more than you do. He wants to help you more than you want to help him! Most of all, place all of your efforts in his hands. He is the source of our evangelization, and we want to make sure that we don't try to do it all by ourselves.

DAY 34—HOW

I love stories because they give us examples that are inspiring and uplifting, but there's also the danger of feeling like they are impossible standards to live by. You might think, "I'm not a traveling evangelist like St. Paul," or "I don't have a deep spirituality like Jan Tyranowski," or "My pastor doesn't like evangelization like Kevin's does." While I hope you found those stories helpful, it's important to realize that you are called to live out your own story. The model of WIN-BUILD-SEND isn't accomplished in one way only.[7] Ultimately, WIN-BUILD-SEND is a mindset and a vision for helping others to come to know Jesus, to live their lives dependent on him, and then send them out to help others do the same. One size definitely doesn't fit all!

Remember, you are called to be an everyday disciple who encounters Jesus, follows him, and makes disciples of others. While you can use some of the example stories given earlier, feel free to work within your own situation or state in life.

In this chapter, I want to show you that WIN-BUILD-SEND can be lived out in multiple ways and to give you some ideas on how you can make it happen in your own life.

WIN

WIN is all about creating moments of encounter with our Lord, just as we saw in week 1. Many of our Protestant brothers and sisters know this step well. They are constantly looking for ways to present the Gospel and help people accept Jesus Christ as the

Lord of their lives. As Catholics, we are often quick to skip this step or don't know how to pull it off. Sometimes we assume that because someone grew up Catholic or attends Mass, they have encountered Jesus. In reality, we should never assume that even the most faithful members of our parish don't need an ongoing encounter. We are never done being won over by Jesus.

Below are some ways to develop a culture of encounter, if we orient these events to a clear presentation of the Gospel and give people a chance to respond:

- Create a parish mission
- Put on a retreat
- Lead a faith study like Alpha
- Invite people to Catholic conferences or to do works of mercy
- Share our life through friendships

The sacraments also provide a valuable way to share the Gospel:

- Marriage preparation and specifically the role of a mentoring couple offers opportunities to share the faith and call others to conversion as they make this big step in their life.
- Likewise, we can present the Gospel during baptismal prep as couples learn how to be parents and bring their children into the Church.
- We can also dynamically share the faith during preparation for first Communion, first Reconciliation, and Confirmation.

BUILD

Once we have encountered Jesus, we need to follow him. As Jesus' disciples, we must "drop our nets" and change the way that we think and live. As we saw in week 2, Jesus didn't send the disciples to a class on his teachings. They didn't take a course or go through a program; they followed him. They lived with him. They watched him. They asked him questions.

When it comes to this step, we often turn to programs as a way to build people up in the faith. But as we saw earlier, programs are most effective in conjunction with a personal connection, or accompaniment. The most effective way for people to grow in the faith is to be in a relationship with others who are trying to do the same. The relationship provides a model for growth, quick advice, and accountability for the journey, just as Jesus provided.

Small-group Bible studies or systems of mentorship can help with this. Make sure the people leading these groups have had an authentic encounter with Jesus and are living an abundant life in him. Note: Many of the BUILD activities below can be used for the WIN stage as well.

WAYS TO HAVE BIBLE STUDIES OR FORMATION IN SMALL GROUPS

- RCIA programs—Open them up to Catholics and non-Catholics who want to learn about the faith.
- Young moms' groups—These groups meet a genuine need for fellowship and support at a particular time of life and also build up others in the faith.
- Young adults' Bible study—Young adults can be strong leaders in your parish. A specific Bible study for them helps them rally together to reach others in your community.
- Married couples' Bible study—Once children come into the picture, these groups can be difficult to continue. One way I've seen them succeed is to make each week different. One week the wives meet. One week the husbands meet. One week all couples meet. One week is an off week.

- Men's groups—These groups are important in encouraging men to be the spiritual leaders of their families and to influence their communities.

SACRAMENTAL ACCOMPANYING

- RCIA sponsors—In her wisdom, the Church created a model of accompanying for new Catholics. This is a good way to mentor others.
- Godparents and Confirmation sponsors—These are two more ways that the Church has incorporated mentoring within its structure. These roles, if taken seriously, can contribute to making disciples and evangelizing others.
- Parents—As they seek the Sacrament of Baptism for their children, parents are called to help their children encounter our Lord and follow him.

To be incorporated into the WIN-BUILD-SEND model, the activities above *must be done with intentionality*. You must be willing to use each activity to spread the faith and continue to mentor people through the process until they are able to do it with someone else.

SEND

Finally, we can't be satisfied with just winning people to the faith and building them up. Remember Pope Paul VI's "test of truth": people who accept the Word must proclaim it to others. For many Catholics, this is the crucial last step that is missing. If we have truly encountered the Lord and others have modeled the faith for us, then we will want to do this for others. It becomes unthinkable not to. This last step becomes a reality when we are intentional about taking it. In *The Joy of the Gospel*, Pope Francis states, "In *all its activities* the parish encourages and trains its members to be evangelizers" (*Evangelii Gaudium*, 28, emphasis added).

Just as we accompanied people through the WIN and BUILD stages, we also need to show them how to provide this encounter and accompaniment for others until they can take people through the WIN-BUILD-SEND process themselves. Typically we mentor them as they begin to lead others through the WIN and BUILD stages themselves.

THE PARISH: AN OASIS

If we live out the WIN-BUILD-SEND model, what is possible for our parishes? In *The Joy of the Gospel*, Pope Francis goes on to say that if we train Catholics to evangelize, the parish becomes "a community of communities, a sanctuary where the thirsty come to drink in the midst of their journey, and a center of constant missionary outreach" (*Evangelii Gaudium*, 28).

What a beautiful image for our Church! In a world where so many people deeply long for God, the Church can become an oasis in the desert where the thirsty are quenched. Enacting the vision of WIN-BUILD-SEND makes this possible.

REFLECTION

Now's the time to think about what you want to do with what you've learned in this book. Reflect on your own situation. How is God calling you to live out the model of WIN-BUILD-SEND as an everyday disciple? You don't need to know every detail to every step of your plan. In fact, you should concentrate on the best place to get started and see how things grow organically from there.

DAY 35—WALK

Over the last five weeks, you have gone on a journey on what it means to be a disciple of Jesus Christ in your everyday life. As we close this book, one of the last remaining questions is, What prevents us from living out Jesus' life and mission? I experienced some hesitation in writing this book and continue to have feelings of inadequacy as I look at Jesus' mission more closely and compare my own life to it. While I have experience with evangelization, I don't write as an expert, but rather as someone on a journey to be more like Jesus.

Often, my reluctance centers on my own failings. I am sinful, weak, ill-equipped, lazy, fearful, and complacent. I am nowhere near who Jesus wants me to be and can't fathom how I could be like one of the many saints in this book. I quickly come up with myriads of excuses. I rationalize that this whole thing just isn't for me. But, as we have done many times in this book, I turn back to Jesus for answers.

IT'S A GHOST!

In chapter 14 of the Gospel of Matthew, the disciples encounter an odd sight. A few hours before, Jesus had told them to go to the other side of the lake while he went off alone to pray. Then, during the fourth watch, sometime between 3 and 6 a.m., the disciples see Jesus walking on water. The disciples have seen a lot of crazy things, but this one has to be the strangest. What would you think if you were in a boat in the middle of the night, and you saw someone walking on water? Fortunately, Matthew captures their reaction in all of its glorious detail: "But when the disciples saw him walking on the sea, they were terrified, saying, 'It is a ghost!' and they cried out for fear" (14:26).

Jesus walking on water is an odd sight, but what happens afterward is even stranger. After Jesus calms the disciples, Peter, in his usual way, steps up and says, "Lord, if it is you, bid me come to you on the water" (14:28). It's amazing that Peter not only thinks of this idea but also attempts it. But, if you think about his training, he had been taught to do everything that the rabbi does. If his rabbi can walk on water, why shouldn't he? And sure enough, Jesus says, "Come."

We all know what happens next: "So Peter got out of the boat and walked on the water and came to Jesus; but when he saw the wind, he was afraid, and beginning to sink, he cried out, 'Lord, save me.' Jesus immediately reached out his hand and caught him, saying to him, 'O man of little faith, why did you doubt?'" (14:29–31).

WHY DID YOU DOUBT?

Notice that Jesus doesn't say to Peter, "Why did you try that, you idiot?" or "What were you thinking? You can't do what I do." No, he tells Peter to have more faith. Our belief in Jesus is intimately tied to our efforts to be like him. It is our ultimate test. Are you willing to walk out on the water?

Even when you fail, when you are weak, when you think you can't do it, Jesus is there to help. (Don't forget the many times that Peter would mess up after this!) Jesus believed in his first disciples, and he chose them to carry out his mission to make disciples of all nations, despite their sins and weaknesses. He does the same with you. He believes in you. He chooses you. And he places his mission to reach the entire world in your hands. Your job is to get out of the boat and walk forward. You are called. Trust in him!

REFLECTION

You have been on quite a journey over the last thirty-five days. More than anything, my prayer is that God has moved in your life and brought you closer to him and his mission.

Take some time in prayer to consider what has impacted you most during this journey. What are your biggest takeaways? How will they change the way you live? Write these down in your journal or even in this book. Find someone who can help you accomplish them and keep you accountable.

ACKNOWLEDGMENTS

To my wife, Lisa—thank you for all of your love, support, and feedback throughout this project. I'm so grateful to live this life with you!

To my parish and to the people I get to work with each week on evangelization (you know who you are)—thank you for your yes!

To my editor, Kristi McDonald—thank you for all of your hard work to make this book what it is. It was a joy to work with you on this project!

NOTES

INTRODUCTION

1. V General Conference of the Bishops of Latin America and the Caribbean, Concluding Document, *Aparecida*, 13–31 May 2007, 6.2.1, paragraph 278.

WEEK 1—ENCOUNTER

1. Augustine, *Confessions*, bk. 8, chaps. 6, 15.

2. For more on the Jewish education system and discipleship, see Ray Vander Laan, "Rabbi and Talmidim," That The World May Know, accessed January 23, 2018, https://www.thattheworldmayknow.com/rabbi-and-talmidim.

3. "How Does God Guide Us?" *The Alpha Film Series*, Episode 7.

4. Thomas Aquinas, *Opuscula 57*, 1–4.

5. Thérèse of Lisieux, *Histoire d'une ame*, "Souvenirs et conseils," p. 263.

6. Marie Kondo, *The Life-Changing Magic of Tidying Up: The Japanese Art of Decluttering and Organizing* (Berkeley, CA: Ten Speed Press, 2014).

WEEK 2—DISCIPLE

1. For more on the Gospel of Matthew and this theme, see Curtis Mitch and Edward Sri, *The Gospel of Matthew* (Grand Rapids, MI: Baker, 2010).

2. Paul Harvey, "The Man and the Birds," *Everyday Christian*, December 17, 2010, accessed February 24, 2018, http://www.everydaychristian.com/blogs/post/christmas_classics_the_man_and_the_birds_by_paul_harvey.

3. For more on the Christ in the City missionaries, see their website: https://christinthecity.co.

4. Gary A. Anderson, *Charity: The Place of the Poor in the Biblical Tradition* (New Haven: Yale University Press, 2013).

5. Andrea Tornielli, "Chaput: 'It Isn't Possible to Be Pro-Life and Simultaneously Forget the Cries of the Poor,'" *Catholic News Agency*, last updated January 2018, https://www.catholicnewsagency.com/news/chaput-it-isnt-possible-to-be-pro-life-and-simultaneously-forget-the-cries-of-the-poor-83859.

6. Augustine, *Sermo* 56, 6, 9: PL 38, 381.

WEEK 3—VISION

1. Joseph Ratzinger, "Homily of His Eminence Cardinal Joseph Ratzinger Dean of the College of Cardinals," April 18, 2005.

2. Flavius Josephus, *Antiquities of the Jews*, bk. 18, chap. 1, 1–6.

3. Flavius Josephus, *Antiquities of the Jews*, bk. 17, 42.

4. Charles J. Chaput, *Strangers in a Strange Land: Living the Catholic Faith in a Post-Christian World* (New York: Henry Holt, 2017), 221.

5. Ralph Martin is very helpful in analyzing this topic. He states, "It is necessary to keep these two truths together, namely, the real possibility of salvation in Christ for all mankind and the necessity of the Church for salvation" (*Will Many Be Saved? What Vatican II Actually Teaches and Its Implications for the New Evangelization* [Grand Rapids, MI: Eerdmans, 2012], 5). This book is an excellent resource on what the Catholic Church teaches about hell, salvation, and the need for evangelization.

6. Martin, *Will Many Be Saved?*, 14.

7. Teresa of Calcutta, *Come Be My Light* (New York: Image, 2007), 26.

8. Teresa of Calcutta, *Come Be My Light*, 27.

9. Teresa of Calcutta, *Come Be My Light*, 41–43.

10. Teresa of Calcutta, *Come Be My Light*, 42.

11. Teresa of Calcutta, *Come Be My Light*, 47.

12. Gary A. Anderson, *Charity*, 5–6.

WEEK 4—EQUIPPED

1. Benedict XVI, "Homily for Eucharistic Celebration on the Occasion of the 23rd World Youth Day," July 20, 2008.

2. Robert Claude, *The Soul of Pier-Giorgio Frassati* (Cork: Mercier Press, 1960), 17.

3. Claude, *The Soul of Pier-Giorgio Frassati*, 17.

4. Claude, *The Soul of Pier-Giorgio Frassati*, 28.

5. Harriet Sherwood, "Nearly 50% Are of No Religion—But Has UK Hit 'Peak Secular'?" *Guardian,* May 13, 2017, accessed January 24, 2018, https://www.theguardian.com/world/2017/may/13/uk-losing-faith-religion-young-reject-parents-beliefs.

6. "Alpha Course Pioneer Nicky Gumbel," filmed July 28, 2009. YouTube video, 2:20. Posted July 2009, https://www.youtube.com/watch?v=ZUHPfvCToCk).

7. "Alpha Course Pioneer Nicky Gumbel," 2:46.

8. Alpha, "Our Story," accessed February 24, 2018, https://alphausa.org/our-story.

9. Alasdair MacIntyre, *After Virtue: A Study in Moral Theory, Second Edition* (South Bend: University of Notre Dame Press, 1984), 216.

10. Chaput, *Strangers in a Strange Land*, 219.

11. Images and content used with permission of FOCUS, the Fellowship of Catholic University Students, www.focus.org.

12. Another great way to share the kerygma is a booklet called *The Ultimate Relationship*, by Catholic Christian Outreach. They've influenced FOCUS's work on the Crux, particularly questions about where someone is in their relationship with Jesus and where they want to be.

WEEK 5—DISCIPLE-MAKERS

1. For more on this exponential growth, see Curtis Martin, *Making Missionary Disciples: How to Live the Method Modeled by the Master* (Genesee, CO: FOCUS, 2018).

2. Christian Smith, Kyle Longest, Jonathan Hill, and Kari Christoffersen, *Young Catholic America: Emerging Adults In, Out of, and Gone from the Church* (New York: Oxford, 2014), 198.

3. Quoted in George Weigel, *Witness to Hope: The Biography of John Paul II* (New York: HarperCollins, 1995), 168.

4. Andre Frossard, *"Be Not Afraid!": John Paul II Speaks Out on His Life, His Beliefs, and His Inspiring Vision for Humanity* (New York: St. Martin's Press, 1984), 18.

5. Weigel, *Witness to Hope*, 60.

6. Clare Anderson, "The Tailor-Mystic Who Inspired a Pope," *Faith Magazine*, March–April 2014, accessed January 24, 2018, http://www.faith.org.uk/article/march-april-2014-the-tailor-mystic-who-inspired-a-pope.

7. For more on WIN-BUILD-SEND, see Martin, *Making Missionary Disciples* (2018).

KEVIN COTTER is the executive director of The Amazing Parish and served as senior director of curriculum at FOCUS, where he worked for eleven years. He earned a bachelor's degree in religious studies and philosophy from Benedictine College and a master's degree in sacred scripture from the Augustine Institute.

He is the author of five books, including *Dating Detox*, which he coauthored with his wife, Lisa.

Cotter has appeared on Catholic radio and television, including EWTN, Relevant Radio, Immaculate Heart Radio, and on SiriusXM's The Catholic Channel. His work has been featured on a variety of Catholic websites, including *Denver Catholic*, *National Review*, *Catholic Exchange*, and *Life Teen*.

He lives with his family in the Denver, Colorado, area.

FR. MIKE SCHMITZ is a priest of the Diocese of Duluth, where he serves as director of youth and young adult ministry for the diocese.